God Bless!

FOLLOWING YONDER STAR

Following Yonder Star
The Untold Trials of the Three Kings
By Martin Gibbs

FOLLOWING YONDER STAR: THE UNTOLD
TRIALS OF THE THREE KINGS

Martin Gibbs

© 2012 Martin Gibbs

ISBN: 978-1475080605

To Dori, always and forever.

Contents

Part III: Behold Him Arise

Foreword

This little story of historical fiction is part adventure, part lesson, and part prayer. Inspired by Matthew and an old English volume titled *Historia Trium Regum* (*The Three Kings of Cologne*), the following is an account of a perilous and miraculous journey to Bethlehem.

While the full veracity of John of Hildesheim's account is uncertain, the story of the three kings has fascinated mankind for two centuries and will continue to do so. What I have attempted in this story is to put a detailed backstory to the journey that the three men endured, thereby adding power to the nativity itself, and elevating the star of Man to a higher level. The story encourages determination, courage, strength, dedication, and most of all, faith.

I hope you enjoy the journey.

Matthew 2:1-12

After Jesus had been born at Bethlehem in Judea during the reign of King Herod, suddenly some wise men came to Jerusalem from the east asking, "Where is the infant king of the Jews? We saw his star as it rose and have come to do him homage."

When King Herod heard this he was perturbed, and so was the whole of Jerusalem. He called together all the chief priests and the scribes of the people, and enquired of them where the Christ was to be born.

They told him, "At Bethlehem in Judea, for this is what the prophet wrote:

'And you, Bethlehem, in the land of Judah, you are by no means the least among the leaders of Judah, for from you will come a leader who will shepherd my people Israel.'"

Then Herod summoned the wise men to see him privately. He asked them the exact date on which the star had appeared and sent them on to Bethlehem with the words, "Go and find out all about the child, and when you have found him, let me know, so that I too may go and do him homage."

Having listened to what the king had to say, they set out. And suddenly the star they had seen rising went forward and halted over the place where the child was.

The sight of the star filled them with delight, and going into the house they saw the child with his mother Mary, and falling to their knees they did him homage. Then, opening their treasures, they offered him gifts of gold and frankincense and myrrh.

But they were given a warning in a dream not to go back to Herod, and returned to their own country by a different way.

Part I
A Journey Begins

Before we ever embark on a journey, there are often smaller journeys that are taken. Getting those last groceries, filling the tank with gas, buying ice, etc. We often forget about these small trips because we think they have nothing to do with the real event.

Do not underestimate the impact even a small expedition may have upon your life experiences. While two of the Three Kings will have significantly harder journeys before their "big one," the moral of the story is that we should always be open and ready to receive, even if we are checking our oil before a long road trip.

When the goal of the journey is neither to return nor to arrive at the scheduled stop, anything is possible.

Chapter 1
Chance Encounter

Again I saw that under the sun the race is not to the swift, nor the battle to the strong, nor bread to the wise, nor riches to the intelligent, nor favor to those with knowledge, but time and chance happen to them all.

Ecclesiastes 9:11

...And the voice of all mothers whispered, "Thanks be to God."

Even the waves lapping the dock seemed dry and dusty. There had been a town here once. now only red sand remained: red, choking, swirling dust, and a few huts collapsing to the dead ground. The dock was rickety, but it held the two boats that slipped ashore. From their sun-seared decks, two well-dressed men emerged, squinting at the harsh light. As the dust swirled around them, their bleached-white garments quickly dulled and streaked with brown sand.

"Nothing!" exclaimed a strange voice. "Nothing here. There is nothing!" The stranger had been watching the boats arrive and rushed to greet the two men warmly. Though his tone had a vein of bitterness, he forced a smile upon his bronzed face.

The newcomers were still wobbly from the route across the wine-red sea and returned his smile with a little effort. After seeing the barren waste where a burgeoning harbor was purported to be darkened their outlook, they scowled at the wasteland beyond.

"Certainly," one of the men started, his voice hoarse. He scanned the desolate area, then cleared his throat, and cracked his knuckles. "I am Jaspar. I rule a little kingdom across the sea called Tharsis."

"I had thought Ethiopia, or from D'Mt," the bronzed man said, his voice inquisitive and scholarly, far from condemnatory. "I am Balthazar. They call me King of Saba, a few hundred miles to the north and east—well, closer to a thousand, but who is counting?" He chuckled, taking another look at the bleak surroundings. "And you are...?" He nodded politely to the third man. "Are you both together?"

"No, we arrived by chance," the third man replied, chewing his bottom lip. "I am Melchior, King of Nubia."

He forced a smile, but the look of disappointment weighed heavy on his features.

"Nubia!" the man exclaimed, with a raised eyebrow— this newcomer could not possibly be a Nubian, his skin was too light. Still... he seemed friendly enough, if not a little bitter at the circumstances. The man on the dock smiled. "I have not had the pleasure, but have heard wonderful things." He thumbed his earlobe and smiled. "But you travel alone with no retainers, apart from your boatmen?" he wondered.

Jaspar and Melchior nodded. Jaspar opened his mouth to explain, but Balthazar was already talking. He seemed a natural leader, a free talker, and one who was quick with a smile, even after a long journey to find nothing. He glanced back at his single man tending to the camels and smiled.

"Traveling, it is therapeutic," the leader of Saba said. The others agreed with polite mutters. "Riding alone can clear the mind. It gets me away from all of the questions and the noise—but this journey, it was not so fruitful." His voice had an edge of giddiness to it, as if he were covering his disappointment. Perhaps he had *hoped* to find nothing.

"I was told there were fruit trees and an oasis ready for trading! How disappointing," Melchior said. "But as you say," he added, looking up into Balthazar's twinkling eyes, "it is a rare pleasure to travel alone and to look at the stars for more than just direction!"

But as he looked up, the king of Nubia's gaze met joy, wonder, and surprise. "You do not view the stars as merely guideposts on your journeys?" Balthazar wondered, his voice a whisper.

Jaspar smiled. "I often wonder what it would be like to travel to a star," he said softly, though his deep voice resonated. "To move through the great void of the night with ease and seek whatever is there…"

The king of Saba beamed. He spread his arms and asked more questions about the stars and the universe… it was not long before the three kings chattered like ancient friends. Their collective interest in astronomy opened up a floodgate of conversation, and they passionately discussed the possibility of other worlds, other realities, and the overwhelming vastness of the sky above.

"So how many stars *are* there?" Jaspar wondered aloud.

"Oh, many more than we can count or even see, I'm sure."

Only two more visitors disembarked during their conversation. Balthazar told them they must have received misinformation, but he didn't receive a word of thanks. Instead, the strangers nodded to Balthazar, though when their gazes crossed Jaspar, they scowled deeply before floating back into the red sea.

"Countless stars..." Melchior whispered. His prior bitterness at the empty dock had faded, though he still looked downcast.

"To think that God could create so many different and amazing stars..."

"That is what makes it more amazing, Jaspar. That's what makes it... remarkable."

Their conversation stretched for hours, the heat blistering in the square and sweat pouring down their faces. It soaked through their garments, dripped down their backs, and pooled in the bottoms of their sandals. A cough from Balthazar's man shook them out of their reverie—though the day was intense in its heat, it was well past noon, and each had a long journey home. It was sadly well past their time to sail away.

"We must resolve to meet one another," Balthazar said finally. "At the very least, correspond via letter. There is much we can learn and discover—though I live quite far from here, I'm willing to travel and continue these discussions."

They agreed to travel first to Nubia, to gather at Melchior's palace. Four years passed before such a meeting took place, though they sent several letters to one another—often multiple copies of letters to be sure they were not lost or stolen. In another four years, they met in Tharsis, enjoying the hospitality of Jaspar.

$\oint$

As they entered the twelfth year since the first chance encounter, their friendship had blossomed and each ruler eagerly awaited the meeting in Saba, though the journey would be rough for Jaspar and Melchior.

The brutal heat of this twelfth summer had passed by, and Jaspar and Melchior began their preparations for the long and arduous journey to Saba. Though this was their third meeting, there was a different smell to the air, an oddness to the wind, and even the oceans seemed to flow differently. For the kings, it could have likely been their keener sense of the environment, fostered by their letters, or perhaps something else was happening—for each man's heart leapt at the very thought of Saba and the journey that lay ahead.

Chapter 2
Jaspar

When he established the heavens, I [Wisdom] was there; when he made firm
the skies above,
when he established[d] the fountains of the deep…
when he marked out the foundations of the earth,
then I was beside him, like a master workman.

Proverbs 8: 27-30

A fierce sun set slowly over the knobby hills on the horizon, its last bright rays highlighting the craggy peaks like coal-fire spears of light. Long shadows flowed over the rolling hills, though the filtered beams of light were still strong enough to cast a warm glow over the carpet of myrrh trees.

Jaspar looked out past the ornate and high-reaching towers and gazed upon the greenery in an otherwise barren plain—the trees contrasted jarringly with the brown and dusty earth beneath them. Rains were infrequent here, but the trees were hardy enough to grow into solid stone; the trees still used the canvas to spring into vibrancy and grew against all reason. Just out of sight, behind the rolling brown hills, the ocean heaved and sighed its uninterrupted motion. As the sun dipped beneath the hills, so, too, did the first stars of evening flicker to life. And with their pale light against a violet sky, a desert cold crept through the palace.

At last, the bright sunlight dipped below the crests of the hills, casting the world in the grainy fog of twilight. The green on the trees transformed to a dullish brown, and the earth below seemed nearly black. Sun-bleached towers and once-glimmering latticework were now off-white, as if the vibrancy and elegance inside them had decided it was time to rest. Jaspar sighed and returned to his apartments. The night chill was starting to set in and he donned a thicker robe. Ordinarily, he would light a fire, but it was well past the time he should leave Tharsis for Saba. Balthazar waited, and surely Melchior was on his way by now. Though they would stay in Saba for over a month, it would take them longer to get there.

Tharsis. Although often called Thaars by some of the older populace, the great majority of its citizens called the kingdom Tharsis. *Tharsis.* The word sounded funny in his mind, as if it were a place of legend or stories.

"Tharsis," he whispered, and the name sounded even stranger, as if he were trying to extract a tarry substance from his tongue. Yet it was his land, his place of birth and upbringing, and the land he had ruled for two decades. But he hungered not for power, but for knowledge and enlightenment, both in the stars above and texts of the prophets on earth. Jaspar sought answers to questions his subjects would never dare ask—where they fulfilled their daily life with no other objective but survival; he sought the true purpose and meaning of life. And in the stars and the dust of the earth, he was finding little, even though the correspondence with Melchior and Balthazar filled his head with a vast array of wonderful knowledge. Perhaps this year they could discover something yet unknown, something deeper.

A servant shuffled his feet and Jaspar was pulled from his reverie. He smiled and grimaced nearly simultaneously—he was eager to see his friends again, yet he dreaded the arduous journey. He would avoid the large desert on his journey, but in doing so, he would need to sail some thousand miles along its coast through rough waters. He would then dock several hundred miles south of Saba and take an overland route, through a desert (*of course!* he noted with a grimace) before he reached the palm trees of Balthazar's palace. Though he was skilled at traversing the desert, he had never used this particular route before, and he cracked his knuckles nervously at the thought.

Before he bade farewell to his underlings, he made sure to pack a few bundles of myrrh and a few scrolls.

As he neared the rickety boat that would take him across the blood-red sea, a flicker of sadness passed through him. Though he was not close to any of his servants, he still felt a connection to them, a sense that they were his family. That they had not seen him on his way was troubling. Perhaps they would revolt and seize power the moment the wooden craft touched the waves, or the rulers in the arid land of D'mt to the west would at last march into Tharsis and claim it as their own. He had similar fears on his previous journey, but thankfully those left in charge were competent—this time, however, the feeling was stronger and his faith in humanity was stuck in a deep trough.

The sound of waves lapping the dock shook him and he turned to look at the boat. It was like many of the ships of the region, smaller, but constructed to cross bodies of water such as the Red Sea or even greater sections of open ocean. It looked precarious and worn, but it had made countless trips across the scarlet sea, and to ports unknown, always returning with cargo or emissaries.

To Jaspar, the ship looked like a flayed cockroach, with the cloth sail strung out in a triangular shape, attached with various ropes and beams made from coconut wood. Slim and shallow, the boat had a sharp bow and a blunt stern equipped with a rudder for steering. Its captain had dozens of years of experience in these waters and Jaspar marveled as the man lengthened, shortened, and pulled on the various ropes, setting the sail to bending in various directions. Long oars had been unceremoniously tossed next to the port gunwale, and Jaspar doubted he could use them should something happen to the captain.

He sucked in the strange mixture of moist sea air and the hot, dry dust of Tharsis.

"Aye, this dhow will take you safely 'cross." The captain chuckled as he looked up, a long rope clutched in calloused hands. After a few moments, he nodded. "Well, come on, then, majesty. We best catch this wind. Ruhamah is itchin' to go!" he piped, patting the gunwale fondly, before ducking back inside. The captain's disembodied voice floated from behind the massive sail. "Best hop in, majesty!"

Jaspar cast a longing glance back at the sun-seared shoreline and the small black flecks that were the myrrh trees and shook his head sadly. There were still a few hours of daylight, but navigating by night would not be a problem for either himself or the boatman. Still, the coming of evening often triggered a sadness in his heart, an awareness that the brightness and the safety of day were fading into a cold, dark unknown, and Jaspar felt himself falling into a vast chasm. He forced down his rising unease with a quick smile at Tharsis, saluted the horizon, smoothed his garments, and stepped into the boat.

The captain laughed as he untied the mooring rope with one hand and used the other to push a long oar against the dock. He then coiled the rope gently inside the wooden gunwale and set the oar down with a thud. The small boat drifted slowly away from the dock, lurching out into the harbor as the winds caught the cloth.

As the salty sea breeze whipped his turban and set his eyes to watering, Jaspar thought upon his friends' chance encounter those many years ago and how a false rumor and an abandoned city had brought the three men together. Having hoped for a new trading partner, he had never thought he would come away empty-handed, but with a heart full of a treasured friendship. Twelve years had gone by far too swiftly.

Chapter 3
Melchior

And be not conformed to this world: but be ye transformed by the renewing of your mind, that ye may prove what [is the] good, and acceptable, and perfect, will of God.

Romans 12:2

He was small of stature, nearly a head shorter than the average man, yet his frame was solid and muscular; youth covered his face in right angles and tight skin, and the primness of a flourishing beard covered his face. Life beneath a warm and nearly tropical sun had provided a golden sheen to his skin, and large, bushy eyebrows the color of coal hovered over his round, pitch-black eyes. Though almost opaque, they still shone brightly in the hot desert sun. His nose was a round, a bulbous mass that lay flat on his face, and his lips were thick and chapped by both the sun and his constant nibbling at them. Atop his shaven head, he wore a curiously shaped turban, with a high peak over the head and sides that dipped below his chin. He was often likened to the rulers near the Great River to the west, those who had built massive structures in which they buried their dead.

His own father had once said, "I have people living in huts and they bury their dead in monuments twice the size of Nubia!" Still, the resemblance to the men of the west was uncanny, and people who had been to the region were quick to take notice. Though never to his face, such comments were still audible in a long hallway or on a murky evening—there were times when he even heard the word "Pharaoh" come from the mouths of his citizens, connected to a string of words he would never repeat in distinguished company.

Melchior did not appreciate the comparison to those rulers far to the west, though he often dealt with them in trade. They seemed to be consumed with themselves, obsessed with their multitude of gods. Rumors swirled that the mighty kingdoms were crumbling, or had already fallen—men no longer came to Nubia sporting his style of turban; they looked more like carelessly wound cloth around their pates. Further, the merchants looked more Greek or Roman in appearance. Melchior was glad for the revenue and dared not question the state of affairs with too great an interest. He had no desire to expose Nubia to more invaders.

Melchior held his hands to his face and frowned a shallow frown. He was much lighter-skinned than any of the citizens of Nubia—it seemed every generation in his family displayed progressively lighter skin. While the family had some members who were from the far west, the influence on appearance could not have been enough to lighten his skin so drastically, could it? The ruler of Nubia shrugged and decided to concentrate on the task at hand, when a night-dark servant passed in the hall, and his frown deepened.

"Why am I thinking of this?" he muttered, then smoothed his robes and turned his gaze outside.

Looking out at the gently swaying palm trees, a brief sense of contentment and peace fluttered through his heart, though it evaporated with the first flash of warm, filtered sunlight between the spiny leaves of the trees. His heart stuttered as he reminded himself it was past time that he should be taking his leave. Which meant he had to cross the sea.

Thoughts of the bobbing and swirling ocean set his stomach lurching. It was customary to travel at night in this climate, but his boatman refused to let his "majesty" guide the boat by the stars; Melchior was not sure what would be worse, not seeing the rolling waves by night or seeing them in their vivid horror during the day. Though Melchior could easily navigate by using the stars alone, he graciously allowed the seasoned seamen the opportunity to escort him across the wine-red sea, for ocean travel was still something he was forcing himself to grow accustomed to.

"Pardon me, Majesty," a servant muttered as he brushed by Melchior in order to clear away the teapot and cups from a low table.

"Yes, thank you, thank you," he replied, chewing his lip.

The man worked swiftly, taking care not to clank the vessels together. Melchior watched the man casually and returned a nod as the servant bustled out of the room. Melchior's retainers were few, but they were devout. At least, they pretended to be. It was dangerous to worry about who might not support you fully, for it created an atmosphere of distrust and a level of stress he didn't want to deal with. He would prefer to be seen as wise and knowledgeable, rather than heavy-handed or dictatorial, though he knew it could cost him his rule very easily.

With a sigh, he rolled up his own scrolls and made his way to his camel for the short ride to the ocean. A mule rode alongside, pulling a half-loaded cart—his provisions were meager, barely enough to sustain him on the long journey to Saba, for he would have to cross the red-colored sea and find new animals when he disembarked. Even after such a crossing, he still had countless miles of harsh desert to cross before he reached the lush kingdom of Saba. He hoped on this journey he could avoid the sandstorms that befell him on his journey to Tharsis, but who knew what a strange and new desert would hold? In his letters, Balthazar assured him the trek was well marked and the path known, and that there were many strong and trustworthy men who could guide him, as long as he paid. And he would be paying in gold.

"It will be quiet without you, Majesty," came the soft and care-worn voice of his personal servant. Melchior was checking the various straps on the cart, making sure everything would hold fast for the bumpy ride and hadn't heard the man's soft footsteps.

"I imagine it will," he said, standing and straightening. Already he felt a slight tinge of soreness in his back. It was going to be a very long expedition indeed. "It may be many months before I return, as the last time, but I trust you will maintain order here."

The servant nodded. "Of course."

"Thank you." Keeping order would possibly prove to be more challenging than brushing away the constant layer of dust or polishing bright dinnerware. Those who wanted to usurp Melchior's position would surely see this as an opportunity to wiggle their way into the palace, or hoist upon themselves a shadow of authority. Traveling without his retinue of servants would delay such action for several weeks. Or so he hoped.

If the majority of observers still saw his palace full of activity, they would assume his presence there. However absent he may be from the public profile, he hoped others would think he were ill or not holding any audience. Unfortunately, this would only delay events he was sure were already planned. Those who wished to seize his kingdom would be waiting and ready for the opportunity.

An opportunity he was handing to them on a golden serving dish.

"Is the—is the heavy cargo loaded?"

The servant nodded. No need to put dangerous thoughts into any ears that may be eavesdropping. His "heavy cargo" was a load of gold, part of a stockpile his family had inherited countless years ago—some of his relatives claimed it came from Alexander the Great's own coffers.

"And, Your Majesty?" A look of sadness passed over the man's face.

"Yes?"

"You will be missed."

Melchior looked into the man's deep brown eyes and sighed. He would miss him, too, along with the rest of his staff, his own bed, the green palm trees, and the constant sighing of the wind. As he looked at his servant, a sudden, profound feeling of loss flooded through him. He had traveled away before and never felt any sadness, but now there was something boiling to the surface, something deeper. A melancholy—no, a sense of grief. He felt as if he would never see this person again, and yet his deep sadness did not touch his own person, but instead manifested itself as a heavy and absolute empathy for the wiry man who stood in the sun. What would happen to him? They had veritably grown up together, and though they could not be considered friends by the social strata of their kingdom, they were still close.

With a gesture that was unlike any a king should undertake, he reached out and embraced the man. When they separated, tears flowed freely down each man's cheeks. Melchior turned abruptly and continued to inspect the equipment, while the servant steeled himself and turned back to the palace.

The soft breeze slowly dried Melchior's tears.

Chapter 4
Balthazar

Do not marvel at this, for an hour is coming when all who are in the tombs will hear his voice

John 5:28

Balthazar said a quiet prayer for his friends, then added one for Saba, something he'd been doing often lately. His heart fluttered with nervousness—his long-awaited meeting with Melchior and Jaspar would be soon; they should be here within a month or so. His servants reminded him he had nothing to fear, for it was not his turn to travel, but his burden felt heavier, for he could do nothing but wait. The others could run faster, spur camels, or paddle boats faster. Balthazar was stuck inside his palace with no ability to make time go faster or shrink the distance.

Nervous energy filled him often, and he found it difficult to concentrate. His gaze always seemed to look to the west and south, darting back and forth as if trying to see his companions as they ventured out into the wilderness. *A month out,* he reminded himself, *at least. Relax.* But he could not sit still.

His palace bustled with servants, messengers, and even envoys from other realms, and the whirl of activity only added to the nervous energy, laced with irritation. Several days passed in a blur and he found himself wishing he were traveling and not sifting through mindless tasks. But even as the bustle quieted in the evenings and Balthazar was left in relative silence, the dead quiet was not much solace, either. He fidgeted.

The King of Saba settled himself momentarily into a soft couch, then stood with a groan. He was of medium build and muscular—in his youth, his father did not let him sit idle in his palace. Instead, he required Balthazar to assist in the harvest of frankincense. Though his shifts were shorter than the regular workers, he was still expected to work as hard as any man. The work ethic had done him good, and he still sported a strong frame; his arms were strong ropes of muscle and his legs were hard and sinewy. Living in the sun-drenched climate of Saba lent a glowing bronze hue to his skin, which set off his narrow green eyes. His ancestors had come from deeper in the eastern world and his closest servant often remarked that Balthazar's looks alone were responsible for Saba's successful trade along the silk road and with the Hans to the far east. Balthazar chuckled at that; he hoped rather that his skills as a diplomat and negotiator were the key reasons he had kept Saba afloat. His appearance was nothing to envy: a nose, broken by a snapping tree branch, angled awkwardly along his face, ending at a bushy mustache that capped off a set of thin, pensive lips. Balthazar was easy with a smile, and it took up most of his face.

Balthazar's palace was an enormous, sprawling manse; curved towers reached to the bright blue sky, and gilded trim covered the sun-bleached plaster like a glittering golden spider web. The sprawling estate overlooked a complex system of gardens, separated by low walls and complete with small runnels for irrigation. The incense-bearing Boswellia trees took up a large portion of the landscape and a heady fragrance wafted over everything, covering the land with its sweet, cloying aroma that not only clung to nostrils, but to skin as well, leaving bare skin feeling as if covered in a sticky slime. Balthazar would bathe daily in a clear pool, but each time he emerged, the scent seemed to stick to him like a film, especially during harvest time, when the trees sported their bulbous and oozing lacerations.

The ruler could still feel the stickiness of the frankincense on his hands—all those years of harvesting the precious commodity. He and the workers slashed at the bark of the trees with long machetes, which allowed the resin to bleed out of the tree and harden. Balthazar thought back with fondness on his father's words as he showed his young son the harvesting process: the best resin was that which was nearly opaque, and one had to constantly be on the lookout for the small red-speckled beetles that could take up residence in the trees. Once the goo solidified, it was collected by the workers. They called their job picking up the tears, since the trees looked like they were weeping from their gaping wounds. Yet no matter how scarred the trees became after the harvest, they recovered easily; Boswellia were strong enough to grow in solid rock, so the humid climate in this region of Saba provided a fertile ground in which they could flourish.

Many of the trees out in the field were seventy years old or more, and the youngest were just reaching nine or ten seasons. It took at least ten years of growth in this climate for the trees to bear any of the "fruit," thus it took significant access to land and resources to develop a sustainable crop of incense. The royalty of Balthazar's family line ensured such access to the land and its trees.

For now.

As he scanned the horizon, he could almost hear the whisperings among the people, among the hawkers and the rabble. Rumblings of revolution were afoot. It seemed no matter the actions he took, the people viewed Balthazar as a pushover and an easy man to overthrow. He could not understand it, for he ruled with a soft hand and he thought himself a fair judge. But others thought him a star-gazing fool, who spent more time with his head cocked to the sky than focused on the people. Balthazar could somewhat understand their concern, but he felt his efforts had been equally focused on the well-being and quality of life for his people. The accusations were enough to foster a sense of betrayal and fear.

It seemed a new accuser rose up from the rabble each month. He forced himself to listen to them and push down the frustration and irritation at their audacity to challenge a reign that was peaceful and even. Claims were often wholly irrational.

"Majesty, you do not punish equally. In fact, you do not punish at all, it seems," one of the men had said, only last week.

"I punish," Balthazar would reply. "There are men in the cells for robbery, assault, and—"

"Majesty, pardon, but my neighbor is shorting his wares, and yet you do not punish. Such things must be investigated!"

Balthazar breathed a heavy sigh. "Is this the same neighbor with the locked gate?"

"Y-Yes, why?"

"Then how could you see him shorting his goods?"

"I saw him! I looked right—" At that point, the man colored and stumbled out of the audience chamber.

So, trespassing was perfectly acceptable if one was catching a fellow man cheating? Balthazar would send someone to investigate the claim, but so far, this had been the first accusation against this specific merchant. Likely, the accuser had another grudge—and, Balthazar knew, a grudge against him. The phrase "You don't punish enough" seemed to be popping up more and more. The people would have to be careful; if they wished for a more strict ruler, they may get one, and long for the reign of Balthazar.

What is wrong with these people? Everything tended to look better on the other side of a wall—

"The trees on your land are better than mine, and I want them," his father would often say. "They fight and scratch for things they already have. You must always remind them, young man, they are blessed to be ruled in such a way. Many are old enough to have heard stories of our ancestors and their violent ways... You must remind them, always. I repeat, son, always remind them that they are secure."

"But, Father, why do they ask for what they already have?"

"They do not know they have it. Or, they know they have it, and they want more. More, more, more, there is no bridging the gap between more and enough, son."

Balthazar's thoughts were interrupted when a servant bumped his leg and apologized profusely. The king smiled and waved him on his way. *Will he be one of the usurpers? Will he rise up and claim he does not have enough, when he dines well each night?*

Chapter 5
Rugged Wilderness

For he will command his angels concerning you to guard you in all your ways.

Psalm 91:11

Nearly a month after leaving Nubia, Melchior disembarked in the harbor of a strange city. The surroundings reminded him of home, with swaying palm trees, low sun-splashed buildings with domed roofs, the cry of seagulls, and the dull hum of humanity as it bustled in overcrowded and narrow streets. The city sprawled along the sandy shoreline and small docks seemed to be visible in the far horizon; men stood at the ends of many, dropping lines or nets into the black water.

When he stepped from the boat, his legs wobbled and he nearly toppled over onto the dock.

His boatman smiled warmly and offered a furry, steadying arm.

Melchior shook his head and straightened. "My legs were used to the water!" He stood, swaying, feeling ashamed of himself for looking like a shambling drunk.

The captain of the boat kept a strong hand on his shoulder, his demeanor calm and steadying. "Indeed. Now, are you sure you don't need me to go with you overland?" He finally dropped his hand and smiled warmly.

The king smiled back, this time returning the warm clap on the shoulder. "I would not ask a man of the sea to cross a desert. I am sure I will be able to find men to assist me—no, it looks like your skills are needed here. Stay, I will return in a month or two, but if I do not..." He frowned.

The man smiled.

"Have you ever been here before?" Melchior asked. Should he never see this man again, he could accept the formal language. Perhaps only in Saba could he—*no,* he thought bitterly. *I will never escape it.*

"Aye, as a kid once. Big fish here. Big fish. I—it has been some time. It's a long, long way from Nubia!"

"It is," Melchior agreed. He turned his gaze back out to the sea—their path now erased by the rolling of a million waves. Far beyond, the horizon was a thin gray line. It was hard to imagine he had been far enough out where land was invisible.

The men regarded each other for a moment, the boatman eager to be gone and also dreading the departure. In this strange land, it did not seem out of place for them to address each other as equals. Although Melchior would have preferred it that way back in Nubia, it was still refreshing to talk man to man, and not ruler to subject. A knot caught in his throat and he realized this was farewell—perhaps permanently.

Melchior put out his hand, but the large man sniffed away a tear and pulled the king into a bear hug. With the clap of a massive hand, the sailor finally released Melchior and each man went their separate ways: Melchior up the small incline to seek transport across country to Saba, and his boatman along the docks, looking for work. A few yards along the slick dock, Melchior stopped and turned, watching the man go. He shook his head sadly as a white bird squawked overhead. After asking around after reputable guides, he was able to find a couple of men, two camels, and an ancient mule that looked ready to fall over. Melchior was careful to place his gold and valuables in a beat-up trunk, atop which he piled a bundle of ragged-looking garments. With a grimace, he realized great care would be necessary when opening this trunk, especially under possibly watchful eyes of strangers.

$

His traveling guides spoke Latin well enough to converse, although his skills in the language of the conquerors were weak at best. Still, they knew the route to Saba, though it was a dangerous overland route through harsh desert. Melchior nodded grimly, but mounted his camel and followed the men along the winding streets to the northern gate of the city.

And the way was rough.

They passed through dry savannah and outright scorching desert heat, passing only one small village that clung desperately to life against a hillside. Here they refilled their water skins and fed the animals.

Melchior's companions were quiet, kept to themselves, and never hinted at any threats toward his person or his belongings—they seemed as if they were only eager to get him to his destination before scampering back for another escort. They continued traveling by day, which Melchior found quite remarkable, for traveling across such a wasteland, night was the customary time to travel. Melchior said as much as they stopped at the end of another brutal day in the heat.

"Night is cooler, but one is blind—we do know the way... sir?" one of them said.

"You are not aware of how to navigate by the stars?" he inquired.

"We do, but, well, we usually are going only a short distance, and we do not know the entire way to Saba by night." The leader seemed embarrassed, but Melchior smiled.

"Not to worry, I can help you there." He found himself convincing his guides he could help them by using the constellations. They knew the exact distance to travel, and the direction, and Melchior could navigate by the myriad of stars, if told which way to go. The first night of such travel brought with it increased stress, for the guides at first did not fully trust his ability to read stars in the sky; but when they saw familiar landmarks by the light of day, they clapped him on the shoulder and smiled.

"Sandstorm coming!" one of the leaders bellowed. Melchior was riding along, staring at the black earth. Dawn was beginning to break in the far east, but he paid no mind, eager only to stop and rest for a day. His head jerked up at the loud cry and he instinctively looked to the east and the rising sun.

"From the west!" the man bellowed. "Quick, there's a gully over here. Hurry! Hurry!"

Melchior scrambled, fighting his camel and mule in attempts to drag them to the relative safety of the depression in the ground. The escort had called it a gully, but it was little more than a slight dip in the ground, barely deep enough to hold a man.

They held fast to the reins of their animals, tried to shout soothing words at them, but the animals seemed more upset by the shouting and hollering than the wind. One of the men finally grunted and let go of the reins, shrugging as he ducked his head down and collapsed to the earth. Surprisingly, the animals bowed their heads and turned to the east, letting their backsides take the brunt of the storm. They had apparently been through such conditions before.

The storm was relentless; great howling gusts raged across the barren ground, carrying sand-filled clouds that, with their velocity, stripped the paint easily from sections of exposed carts. The animals swayed under the power of the squall and Melchior swore he heard them howling against the painful attack of the wind-driven sand, although his entire head seemed to be filled with a roar immeasurably louder than the pound of the surf. Hour after hour, the storm raged, and the men, exhausted from traveling, forced their eyes open, hoping against hope that nature's tirade would finish.

But the hours soon passed into days and the storm showed little promise of easing. Day became night became day in a constant, brown cloud. Melchior's stomach growled in protest, then eventually sucked in upon itself in defeat. The camels would fare better than the humans and the mules were probably dead, he thought as the wind raged overhead.

"I—" Melchior started, but his voice was swallowed by the howl.

The older of his guides looked at him and shrugged.

When at last the storm lessened, the men stood with creaking joints to inspect their surroundings. The men and every last item in the possession was coated in a thick layer of sand and grime. Melchior's chest of gold had been stripped of all its green paint and looked all the more like a wandering hermit's than a king's, which in its own way added to his anonymity, though if the lid had been blown off the chest—

He cut that thought off as they inspected the camels and the mule.

The animals were exhausted, spent from the abuse of the sand and the constant noise. They lost another day in waiting for them to recover, although Melchior was glad for that fact, for they were able to eat some of their dried meat and fish. Although their foodstuffs were sealed as tight as possible, still they were gritty with remnants of sand.

He expected his companions to bristle and even leave him stranded, but they seemed almost comfortable with their situation.

"I've seen worse than that," the leader said, spitting out a granule of sand.

"Is that so?"

"Aye, Baraza and I, we've seen it all, haven't we?" he asked, mouth full of dried fish.

The man named Baraza nodded, his own mouth full. "True that, Loran, true that. Why, you can count yourself lucky we still have the camels. And the mules!" He pointed at the animals. "In one storm we lost them all, had to walk all the way back to our camp—took two days to go ten miles, since our eyes were so full of sand. Then *another* storm came and stopped us again. This is nothing."

Melchior chuckled. "That is good to know."

"A man like you," Loran said, pointing respectfully at Melchior, "probably has never seen desert like this."

"Oh, I've seen deserts and sandstorms, yes," he replied carefully. "When I was younger, we traveled far, far west, even past the Great River. There are tall buildings there, built by thousands of slaves—these buildings reach heights you cannot imagine. Well, I will have to imagine

them, I guess, because we got stuck in such a storm...
We had a larger caravan with bigger carts, but..."

"Aye." Loran looked down as he finished eating and
fell silent. Melchior wasn't sure how to read the man, but
he sensed Loran did not believe him. Here he was,
another rich man being escorted by these men, nothing
more than another wealthy traveler who had little
experience outside of his comforts. But the story *was*
true. His heart dropped a little when he realized he
would probably not get to see those tall buildings in his
lifetime.

At least they trusted him enough to guide them by
night.

$

Several nights passed without incident and they
arrived at last at the edge of a deep and dark forest. He
would miss having easy access to the stars and
constellations—he trusted these men, mostly, and they
were indeed headed north and slightly to the east. But the
edge of the forest loomed at the edge of a long field of
dry and cracking grass, and with it, his unbroken view of
the canopy would be lost.

He sighed. There really was no easy way to Saba, it
would seem. His peaceful journey across the sea had

lulled him into a false expectation and he glowered briefly at the thought, but the thought of Saba stilled his doubts and he trudged forward.

Loran and Baraza paused only a moment before leading their animals along a thin trail stretching into the forest. Once inside the grove, Melchior noticed immediately as dry heat gave way to damp and dank air. He had never been among so many trees and so much vegetation; it felt claustrophobic—towering pine trees, with their rough bark and green needles stretched high above the moss-covered earth, their great canvassing branches stretched out in all directions, fighting for their own particle of sunlight, while casting the forest floor in a dark and filtered light.

Within the forest, his ears were assailed with a variety of sounds and scents he had heretofore not experienced. Hundreds of bird calls, the chitter of squirrels, and the smell of pine and the odd pistachio tree growing among the thickets—for a man used to the hush desert sounds and the rumble of the surf, the noise was startling. Loran and Baraza were oblivious to the sounds, and instead, their glances darted into shadowed corners and in the undergrowth of trees as they searched for danger. A skilled bandit could hide in the desert, but it took little cunning to bury oneself in the thick foliage of a forest.

"Dark in here, eh?" Loran said with a crooked grin.

Melchior nodded. "Now, this I have not seen, I admit. So many trees!"

"At least it's cool, no sandstorms."

"True, true." He bit his lower lip and peered into the gloom. His eyes slowly adjusted to the wan light and he could see farther into the woods, but still the trees stretched out of sight in all directions, the rods of the trunks and fingers of the branches leading endlessly to a blur.

Melchior took some solace in the great woods—he could travel by day through the forest at least. Although, by now his sleep was broken and disrupted—having gone from being awake all night to plodding through forests during the day, he was exhausted. Melchior's dreams were confusing as well, full of swirling white colors, vertical beams of light stretching to the heavens, fountains overflowing with milk and honey, and a spinning wheel of pure light, flashing from a hill in the desert.

In the middle of such a strange dream, the chanting of men's voices rose to such a fever pitch that he sat upright, scanning the forest. His throat caught when his ears still registered the sound.

"Wake up!" Loran whispered harshly, though Melchior's eyes were already wide with alarm.

Through the branches of the pine and poplar, Melchior could see the bobbing orbs of torchlight and hear guttural voices as men chanted in the dark.

"Will they harm us?" Melchior wondered.

"Perhaps, aye," Loran whispered back. He opened his mouth to speak, but the group of torchbearers broke through the bramble and into their campsite.

Though they chanted in an odd rhythm, the group of seven men looked little different than Melchior and his companions. Their clothing consisted of nothing more than tattered cloths and thin, leathery sandals. Their faces, however similar to Loran and Baraza, were lined with determination and upon seeing the strangers in the forest, they gave such looks of loathing that Melchior was at once taken aback. When the strangers raised spears, ogled the travelers, and rubbed their bellies, Baraza whispered in terror, "Cannibals!"

"No..." the King of Nubia whispered.

"Aye," Baraza whispered back, his breath reeking. "They are going to kill us."

Loran had come awake and watched in silence, wringing his hands.

"Did you bring weapons?" Melchior wondered, staring as the natives paused. As one, they traded glances at Baraza and Melchior as they spoke in harsh whispers.

"No, it only invites trouble."

The laugh died in his throat. *No, but not having them has caused quite a great deal of trouble!* Instead, he added, "You've traveled this forest before, haven't you?"

Baraza nodded. "Aye, but this has never happened before, I—"

Melchior shot him a disgusted glance, ready to accuse him of some gross misdeed, but stilled his tongue. His guides were terrified, Loran paralyzed and Baraza near the point of a breakdown. At the pause in their conversation, the natives took notice and advanced a step.

A thought struck Melchior. Standing abruptly, he showed his palms to the advancing men. They paused only a moment before taking another step. "Wait!" he told them, though the word did not register. Melchior quickly loped over to his chest of gold. Opening it, he pulled away the dirty garments, and displayed the contents to the natives, for the moment ignoring the wide stares of Baraza and Loran. "Gold," he whispered. The bright metal glittered in the light of the torches. "Gold, all the gold—"

The natives took a collective step forward, ignoring the glittering of the bullion and coins.

"It's not working," Loran hissed.

Melchior bit his lower lip and closed the lid on the gold-filled trunk. His mind raced through possibilities of escape—normally the gold would be enough to satisfy any bandit. And now that he'd shown his companions his possessions, he had further exposed himself to danger, should they survive this encounter. The natives took another collective step forward; the leader rubbed his stomach and smiled.

God help me.

Melchior gnawed at his bottom lip, glanced nervously at his companions, then at the advancing natives. There was perhaps one more thing he could try—with a prayer to every god he had heard of, he took some coins out of the chest, filling his fist. The natives took a step closer, but he showed them a fistful of the currency and smiled at them. He spoke as though they could understand him and set them down on the ground before him, in the pattern of a star. "See, I lay one here, and one here. And then I step back." He took a step back and pointed at himself and his companions. "We are but three weary and small travelers. Small..." He emphasized, gesturing to his narrow frame. He made another sign with his hands near his stomach, indicating its slimness. Then he pointed at the ground. "With these coins... the coins"— he gestured at the star pattern—"this will bring many more men but bigger!" Melchior pointed up at the sky, then gestured to the west, as if waving someone forward. "Big men!" he added, making a sweeping gesture around his belly. He pointed again at himself and his companies, made a small sign for thinness, pointed at the coins, pointed at the sky, and repeated the signal for a large man. The king then pointed at the coins once more. "These men will come for the coins." Again, he repeated his gesture.

He looked up with hope at the strangers. But his heart sank as they took another step forward. "No, no!" he blurted, pointing again at himself. "You do not want me. I am small and weak. The coins! The coins! They will bring much larger men for you!" Melchior repeated the pantomime, finishing with a smile.

One of the men looked at him, then spoke a few words in his language. In so doing, he aped Melchior's previous gestures, finishing by pointing at the coins.

"Yes, yes, they will bring more men!" Melchior nodded enthusiastically.

The natives paused, then bowed their heads together in fervent conversation. At last, they returned their stares to Melchior and his companions, taking care to inspect every inch of their scrawny frames. Finally, the leader grunted and turned back to his companions. With another snort, he squatted on the ground and uttered a few more words, gesturing again at Melchior, then looked at the coins with a small smile.

"He's telling us to leave," Baraza said. "Look how he points at us and then the forest. Come, let us be gone from here."

Melchior and Loran wasted no time in gathering the few stray belongings and guiding the animals into an unknown blackness. The light of the torches provided a meager guide, but faded quickly as they edged into the deeper void of night. Only when the lights had gone completely black did Melchior let out a heavy sigh.

"That was very smart," Baraza said absently.

"Thank you." *No doubt he is thinking of my gold,* Melchior thought, chewing his bottom lip. *I will have to be very careful... I just wish I could see! How can these men know where they are going? Was I set up? Was—*

His thoughts were broken by Loran's gruff voice. "Worry not, Your Majesty, about the gold. We will tell no one."

His throat seized up, even in the dank environs. "How do you know...?" Melchior wondered.

"For a man to have that much gold, he must be wealthy," Baraza said. "You're not a thief, else you would have left us in the desert after the storm. And you are smart and cunning—people listen to you even though they do not know your language. You must be a king. Though I don't know why a king would leave—"

Melchior nodded. "Yes, I am a king of a faraway land. I am traveling to meet a—" He was about to say he was meeting another king, but another word leapt to his tongue. "Friend. I am meeting a friend. My servants are many, though I needed to be free from everything. Everything. I was hoping for a peaceful journey." He took another backward glance, then laughed heartily.

"Well... we'll do our best to offer you that," Loran said. "From now on, at least. And do not fear for your gold. It is not ours."

Thank you, God, Melchior thought.

He raised his hand in front of his face and chuckled inwardly—he saw nothing. As hard as he stared, the void was solid. Unable to help himself, he laughed again.

"What is it?"

"I—I can't even see my hand..."

Loran and Baraza broke into laughter themselves as they led him through the dark forest, though he knew they were just as blind as he. They continually fought through brambles and large bushes, which forced them to calm already nervous animals. After they had traveled for several hours, they strained to listen for any other sounds. A whippoorwill sang its lonesome song, then went silent, leaving the forest in its muted hum of night.

The next day found them free of the forest and back into a dusty savannah, which itself gave way to another desert, though a worn trail led northeast. "Saba," Loran said, pointing. "Is not far up that road."

"I must thank you both for the escort," he said to the men.

Each nodded and smiled as he handed over the payment, plus a few coins extra. "What's this for?" Baraza asked.

"For the sandstorm, the forest, the cannibals... for carrying my belongings much farther than you probably expected. I cannot thank either of you enough for keeping me safe through this rough journey."

"It was all part of the agreement," Loran said quietly.

"Plus you saved our lives, remember?" Baraza added.

"I—yes, well, we kept one another alive. And I showed you the amount of gold that I carry... and you never made a move to steal from me. For that I wish to repay you."

"I... We cannot take it. Baraza and I, well, this is our job!"

"Take the money."

The men protested heartily, but in the end, they kept the gold, for which Melchior was grateful. He had not paid them nearly enough, he felt. He had thought of striking out on his journey without aid, but he would surely be dead or eaten had it not been for his two guides.

Chapter 6
Sea of Red, Sky of Gray

A generation goes, and a generation comes,
... but the earth remains forever.
The sun rises, and the sun goes down,
... and hastens to the place where it rises.
The wind blows to the south
... and goes around to the north
around and around goes the wind
... and on its circuits the wind returns.

Ecclesiastes 1:4-6

The ride across the sea was short, but nerve-wracking. Jaspar never had much of a liking of the large, red-tinted body of water. The red soil on its banks lent it a wine-colored hue, but farther out, the sea was clear enough to observe fish swimming beneath the boat. Not able to swim, he continuously cast nervous glances at the void that opened up beneath the ragged wooden hull. Death wobbled below, a roiling liquid bed that would claim him should he fall in.

His boatman had only two teeth and laughed at nearly every lurch and drop of the rickety vessel. Surely, he enjoyed the green tint that covered Jaspar's face. "You don't travel the sea much do ye, Majesty?" the man asked, laughing again.

Jaspar held his mouth firmly shut as the boat heaved over another enormous wave.

"Do not fear, Majesty," the man bellowed. "I'll keep ye safe, as best as I can, but be——" An enormous wave broke over the bow, soaking both men. When, at last, the water rushed off the deck and streamed into the sea the man continued as if he had merely swatted away an annoying fly. "Aye, don't ye worry!"

The ruler of Tharsis kept his mouth and eyes tightly closed, but nodded respectfully to the experienced seaman. As another torrent of water cascaded over him, he said a silent prayer for safety and gripped the side of the boat tightly. He thought about going below decks, but grimaced at the thought. The space below was cramped such that a man would be crushed to a pulp from the knocking of the waves. At least here, on top, he could see the waves coming—that is, when he allowed himself to open his eyes. But even the thought of being bundled and cramped into the small space was enough to raise his hackles... As violent and unstable as it was up here, he at least had a grip on the boat and the reassuring words of his toothless captain.

"Storm is lightening up now, Majesty," the seaman called suddenly. Jaspar finally opened his eyes, wiped away the salty moisture, and looked out at the roiling sea. The waves were indeed smaller than before, although the boat still lurched and heaved over a few large swells. Still, the red water appeared to be returning to a calmer state than the crimson monster it had been. At the sight of the changing water, Jaspar lifted his head to the sky and offered thanks; as he did so, more water poured out from his saltwater-soaked tunic.

"Thank God for that," he said, smiling at the boatman.

"Aye, indeed," the man said with a smile.

The red sea rolled lightly for a few more hours, but nothing compared to the violent upheavals they had survived. Jaspar still stood in his soaked garments, waiting for the moment when the water would again boil into a fury and swamp the small boat. But soon, the sun burst through the low clouds and the warmth began drying his shivering frame, though his clothing was still soaked through.

"Land ahead!" the seaman barked, pointing east.

Jaspar squinted, and the thin line on the far horizon slowly developed into the rough contour of the far shore.

He sighed loudly and allowed himself a small smile at the thought of dry land. But the smile faded as he thought on the journey yet to come—he had only traveled a quarter of the distance to Saba.

"Ye best dry those clothes, Majesty... The dust and dirt will stick to 'em surely."

"Indeed, indeed," Jaspar replied quietly. He ducked into the confined space below and clumsily changed his garments. Though the seas had lessened, here in the confined cabin, the rocking felt anything but gentle, and he stumbled in the small moving space. At last, he was able to struggle into dry clothes and make his way up to the deck. The ruler of Tharsis tossed his bundle of wet clothes unceremoniously overboard.

The captain stared. "Ye could have saved them, Majesty, for the return journey."

"No, no," he replied, shaking his head. "Best not burden you with my wet clothes—what is another robe, anyway?" Suddenly, the boat lurched and he had a quick, sickening thought race through his mind. *There are people who cannot afford a single stitch of clothing, and I just tossed a silk garment over the side of a boat...*

"Majesty, are you well?"

"I-I'm fine, I think. I—On second thought, I'm not so sure I should have thrown that—" He turned quickly around to look for the robe floating in the sea, but his gaze only met the deep red hue of the water and the light foam that the boat churned in its wake. "Someone could have used it, surely."

The captain nodded, casting his own glance back to the boat's wake.

By the time the shoreline came into full view, the sun had risen past its peak and was beating down on their shoulders. The dry heat felt good after spending several days sloshing in seawater and being drenched by the overflowing waves; though he wore a fresh set of clothes, Jaspar still felt soaked through to his core, and he relished the burning heat. Again, he closed his eyes and leaned against the gunwale as the small boat lapped slowly toward shore. Only when they thumped lightly against the dock did he open them.

After they had docked and unloaded his belongings, his boatman bid him farewell. Jaspar thought he saw the sparkle of a tear in the man's eye, but he was afforded no time to inquire as the seaman ducked off along the wharf. Jaspar's own stomach felt sick, though no longer from the rolling waves, but from a sense of sorrowful parting.

His journey was hardly easier overland. His guide had found a so-called quicker route to Shiraz and onward to

Saba. The distance may have been less, but the trail they followed was no wider than a man's shoulders. It was pitted, rock-strewn, and muddy in parts. Riding the camels was not an option.

Since the trail was so narrow and unforgiving, there was no opportunity to camp or rest. Jaspar and his leader were hunched over with exhaustion by the time they reached the summit of the low range and began their descent to the flat ground at the base. For two solid days, they walked their animals and gear along the dangerous track and suffered the bite of both the cold starless mountain evenings and large flies by day.

When Jaspar handed the man an extra coin, the guide's eyes went wide. "But…"

"No, take it. This surely would have killed me had I been on my own. I must thank you and hope to work with you again—I know the way now to Saba. Thank you."

The man nodded and returned down the trail.

Chapter 7
Will We Never See Joy?

Is not human life on earth just conscript service? Do we not live a hireling's life? ... I have months of futility assigned to me, nights of suffering to be my lot... Remember that my life is but a breath, and that my eyes will never again see joy.... Suppose I have sinned, what have I done to you?

Job 7:1;3;20

Though this meeting had only been the third they had shared (not counting their first encounter), somehow it seemed to them as if it were the last one they would have. It felt like a last chance for true knowledge and enlightenment, though if asked, none of them would be able to pinpoint why they felt that way.

As he spurred his camel faster toward Saba, Melchior's heart raced with a nervousness he had never experienced. Trying to get a sense of his feelings, he realized that the feeling was something akin to fear, but not terror or horror. He did not fear losing his kingdom, though the citizenry would sure suffer under whatever usurper seized power. For his own life, there was little concern, for he believed in something beyond the sufferings of the living.

It was a fear of the unknown. But that did not fully explain the feeling, either.

He had survived two serious ordeals in this strange land, and his men had stuck with him through both and had made no move to steal his gold. Loran and Baraza had been good men.

"What do I fear?" he wondered of himself. The sound of his voice in the dry air sounded loud and awkward. But again, the feeling of dread and foreboding crawled over him, and he looked out at the barren landscape, seeking answers in the void.

An animal of unrecognizable species lay dead in the trail, though Melchior did not notice until his camel lurched to avoid the rotting corpse; oddly, the desert was void of the sound of vultures. Not even the buzz of flies was audible

Death. I am going to die.

He held his head high and continued.

As Jaspar began his own trek across country, he likewise felt a sense of dread, though he attributed his feeling to his presence in a strange land, his glaringly different physical appearance, and the strange grizzled man who accompanied him. The hired hand, however, seemed to pay little mind to his skin color and cared only for the color of his gold. That the man had been such a mercenary was at once comforting and disconcerting— what amount of gold would set his guide against him?

As he bid the man farewell, he realized his fears were unfounded, for the gruff companion continued westward, and Jaspar watched as his turban vanished over the horizon. With a sigh, Jaspar spurred his animal toward Saba. A few quick glances back along the desolate plain confirmed the man had not followed. So far he knew of no man who could hide in open country. Without any companion, the feelings of desolation and sorrow returned, but coupled with a sudden nervousness.

A boyish apprehension overcame him. Something akin to the feeling of holding a woman's hand, a forbidden pleasure that coursed through his spine, along the backs of his knees, and through is feet, as if he were about to watch a skilled dancer flit across an acre of hot coals or take in a fire-breather at the yearly carnival. Nervousness did not begin to describe his feelings, he realized.

Upcoming discussions on astronomy and the universe held great appeal, and the knowledge he would learn and share seemed limitless. He had found new scrolls, and thereby new knowledge of religions, prophecies, and the state of the world. Surely, Melchior and Balthazar had with them newer items as well, or even new perspectives on older documents and writings. He was excited to learn and teach… but there was another, deeper feeling that permeated his joyousness.

A single bird flew overhead and squawked. His attention was drawn to the bird and then to the landscape slowly becoming more lush and full of life around him. Green shrubs grew in large numbers; grasses could be seen poking through the dry ground, and, after several miles, palm trees were visible in larger numbers. The change in scenery seemed to set the tumblers of thought rolling and he recognized the deep-seated emotion.

It was mourning!

"Now, how could that be…?" he whispered to his camel. What was he mourning? His kingdom? His staff and retainers? As he thought more, he realized it was not a feeling of having lost someone, but the premonition that one is *about* to lose someone. He remarked this with another flutter of his heart.

He rode in silence, eyes glassy as his mind tried to work out the true depth of his lamenting. "I'm mourning myself," he said suddenly. He reached up to feel his beard and mouth—the words came out so rapidly and with little conscious thought that he felt as if something else had moved his jaw.

Myself?

"My own death?" he wondered aloud.

At that, he pulled the camel to a stop. It was too much. The sound of the hooves on the ground, coupled with his own racing mind distracted him from his thoughts. Again, how exactly does one mourn himself?

"I'm going to die, aren't I?" he asked the camel, who in turn only snorted, eager to keep moving.

His gaze was still out of focus when he finally spurred the animal forward. No, he was not going to die—at least not today. *At least not now...* Perhaps he wasn't going to die in the true sense of the word, either. Maybe there was a great change coming that would forever alter his being. He hoped as much, at least. As strong as he could be as a leader, the thought of passing away still set the heart fluttering. *Maybe only a part of me will die. I feel—*

He put words to his thoughts. "I feel as if part of me will die... the Jaspar who left Tharsis is no longer the Jaspar who is here, or who will be."

The camel snorted again.

Chapter 8
Danger in the Garden

Tell your children about it and let your children tell their children, and their children the next generation! What the nibbler has left, the grown locust has eaten, what the grown locust has left, the hopper has eaten, and what the hopper has left, the shearer has eaten. Wake up, you drunkards, and weep! All you wine-bibbers, lament for the new wine: it has been snatched from your lips.

Joel I: 3-12

Balthazar stood atop one of the crenellated balconies and gazed out at his gardens with a faraway look in his eyes. A few years ago, he had traveled across the searing desert and the narrow red sea to visit Jaspar; as he thought about that long journey, he did not envy his companions. Each faced a hard passage fraught with danger. Balthazar balled his fists and unclenched them, looked into his sun-darkened hands, and frowned. He was getting old. If they were to hold their next summit in three or four years, he was unsure if he could be in good enough condition to travel. His last expedition had resulted in the loss of one man, near starvation, and a horde of—

A pain coursed through his hands and he realized he had balled them into fists again. When he was only eight years old, a venomous snake, hiding in the branches of the fragrant trees, had lashed out and snared his hand. Luckily, he did not suffer a large amount of poison, but for several days, he lay incapacitated, lost in the throes of a deep fever. In his fever-dreams, he imagined the snake talking to him, spinning all sorts of wild tales about fruit, apples, and gardens. His parents laughed him off, blaming the poison and the fever.

The sun lifted lazily above the fragrant trees, the bright flashes broke his image of the past. He squinted as if waking from a dead sleep. Morning had changed to mid-morning, and he had done nothing but stare out at his gardens. Hopefully, it would not take much longer for his friends to arrive—as relaxed as he should be, staring at nothing, he felt as if he should be in a hundred places at once, pulled in every direction.

While Melchior and Jaspar struggled to survive rugged seas and unforgiving wilderness, Balthazar sat in his palace, alone as one could be with a sizable staff of servants. This should have afforded him at least a sense of peace and calm, but a singular event occurred, which set his experience on a plane with the trials his companions faced.

Near the end of a long and sweltering day, he wandered out into the gardens for a stroll. The heat had finally melted into cool, rippled with a gentled breeze; the sun's harsh light had faded as the orb dipped below the western horizon, and the comforting shadows of dusk settled over the gardens. After a full day of baking in the sun, the trees gave off their aroma in thick, gummy waves.

As he neared one of the trees, Balthazar heard a slight hissing sound. Instinctively, he stepped away from the tree, thinking the sound came from a snake hiding within the branches. Furtive looks into the branches discovered nothing. He let his eyes travel back to the path in front of him, and as his gaze fell to the ground, he lurched at the sight illuminated by the fading sunlight.

Beetles.

Thousands of beetles—rather, tens of thousands—swarmed along the path in front of him. Father called them longhorn beetles, and they lived within the trees, though the snakes often took care of them. The bugs could be quite disruptive to any wood structure, and Balthazar's thoughts went to his library, constructed partially using large log beams. A great swarm of beetles could easily chew through the wood and destroy the—

They could easily destroy me! His throat caught as the realization hit him He took another step back, and as he did so, the swarm seemed to notice the motion and slithered closer—as one cohesive unit. When he dared step back another foot, the throbbing mass moved again, and he swore the heap grew several inches.

If he had not been almost paralyzed with terror, the sight would have raised his hackles. The longhorn beetle was an ugly creature, with its rough brown-scaled back, tiny black orbs for "eyes," its too-long antennae and hair-covered feelers that stretched beyond the head. Tens of thousands of these creatures slithered, hard shells clicking loudly together. As they crawled over each other, their feelers clacked against other feelers and hard backs, creating a disconcerting throb. Insects. How he disliked these tiny little creatures.

The pulsating pile crept nearer, and he found himself taking another step back. This time, his heel caught the stone trim of a pond and he flipped back into the dark water with a great splash. Though the water had been warmed by the sun during the heat of the day, the shock was still enough to inspire a gasp out of Balthazar.

Having noticed his plight, the mound of beetles oozed toward him, and the dull hiss grew louder. Balthazar tried to push himself upright, but his hands sank into the soft muck at the bottom of the pond and he fell back into the water with another loud splash. It would only be a matter of time before—

He let out a sickening cry as he felt the first few beetles crawl up his leg, skittering northward. They were not biting. Yet. But he feared the worst—that they would slowly devour him where he lay. More of the hideous creatures scrabbled up his other leg and he instinctively kicked outward, trying to throw them off. A few went flying out into the night and he was able to force himself to roll back into the pond and leap to his feet.

The water was up to his waist, but the beetles did not stop at the edge. The mound moved forward and, one by one, longhorn beetles floundered into the water. A few splashed a few moments before going still, but others succeeded in crossing the pond to where Balthazar stood, many now using the bodies of their drowned companions as a bridge. He swiped dozens away and turned to exit on the other side of the pond—but to his horror, the mound expanded outward along the edges of the pool.

"Nador...," he whispered. Clearing his throat, he finally shouted for his servant. Terrified, he stood in the muck of the pond, staring at the throbbing piles of bugs. *What if there were more? What if they had invaded the palace? Where had they come from? And why so many?*

"Nador!" he shouted again.

More beetles tried the path across the water, and soon, Balthazar flailed away at the many scurrying across the surface of the pond. He looked like a mad man, his arms swinging wildly at the water, slashing away the creatures that raced toward him, even slicing at the dead ones. Dark water bubbled in the small pond, and waves created by his furious splashing slammed against the stone-lined edge, spilling up and over. Still, the beetles kept coming. The footsteps of Nador were drowned out by the sound of the violent splashing.

His servant saw the predicament Balthazar was in and sprinted back to the palace. When he returned, he carried a bucket of oil and a torch. Without hesitation, he poured half the bucket over one pile of beetles and dropped the torch on it—with a roar the beetles ignited, crackling in the heat. The fire was accompanied by a stench of death, as if someone had left a roast on the fire for too long. Nador raced to the other pile and ignited them likewise, then reached out to pull Balthazar from the pond.

He was nearly inconsolable as he swatted at his robe—each stray beetle he shook loose was crushed underfoot.

Only after several minutes of swatting and stomping did he straighten out and thank Nador. "I-I don't know—what—what that was!" He panted between each word.

His servant shook his head nervously and swung the torch around the garden. "I've never seen anything like it. That smell!" he exclaimed suddenly. "I—thank God you are alive!"

Balthazar nodded. He still breathed with a heavy exhaustion. The smell filled his nostrils—a metallic, sickly-sweet odor mixed with the smell of char and broiling meat. Nador held his nose and beckoned his ruler inside to where they could lay some herbs atop a roaring fire.

"What *were* those things?" Nador wondered as they sat before the hearth. Nearly an hour had passed since the incident, but each man still cast nervous glances toward the garden, listening for any sound of small scurrying or scratching on the stones.

"Longhorn beetles," Balthazar answered quickly.

"I-I know. I mean, rather, why? Why were there so many? Where did they come from?"

The King of Saba shivered despite the warmth of the fire. "I wish I knew." He stared into the flickering flames for a few moments and then cleared his throat. "Actually...," he began, "it reminds me of a story about locusts and how they destroyed everything—an entire nation, actually, reducing a once-vibrant land to dust."

"Was it a true story?"

"It could've been... yes. Myself, I took it as a warning to not become dependent on earthly things. Even these trees that sustain us can be taken. Perhaps that was a lesson intended for me."

Nador shook his head. "Majesty, if I may be so bold, that was a horrible lesson."

At that, Balthazar laughed. "I could've run swiftly and avoided them... frightening as they were!" *But why didn't I think of it?* He shivered. "But having beetles crawling on your skin is not a pleasant experience. Perhaps it was a lesson I needed to learn. Tell me, Nador," he said suddenly. "Am I a fair ruler?"

"Your Majesty, I—" The servant was surprised at the sudden change of direction, but Balthazar read it as a protestation.

"Please, Nador. Humor me. Am I?"

The servant wrung his hands briefly, then looked up at his king. "You are as fair as your father, if not more so. But..." Nador trailed off, staring at the tile.

"Yes?"

"Maybe... maybe... it is—" He cleared his throat nervously, though Balthazar waited patiently. "You are too fair."

"Too fair?"

"People think they can do anything, and they might get punished, yes, but you never put anyone to death. How can people learn?"

"They can't learn when they are dead," Balthazar replied curtly. "I can't bring myself to such action. I know it's the way of things, and I know there are crimes worthy of death—at least, I'm told there are. I'm not convinced a man or woman can learn and grow if they are killed when they transgress. Do the people truly believe they can commit any crime and avoid punishment? Perhaps they should see the jail—"

"Majesty, they do not fear for their lives, I mean. Apologies for interrupting," he added hastily.

Balthazar waved his hand respectfully. "Why should a man fear for his life in order that he would do good?"

Nador opened his mouth to speak, but closed it slowly. "I fear it is the only threat that many can understand."

"A very smart man, you are, Nador. Perhaps I have misjudged... I thank you for your honesty."

"Thank you, Majesty."

Balthazar yawned and stood slowly. "If you would please excuse me, I would like to be alone. There are some scrolls I'd like to attend to."

Nador nodded and slipped away.

For some time, Balthazar sat in his library, staring at the scrolls. His brain whirled with pieces of fragments of snippets of texts, but he could not seem to focus on any one piece. He kept thinking of the beetles and the locusts, trying to remember the histories on either, but the more he stared at his collection, the more his mind slipped further away from the present. Instead, he sat staring as the fire died down to shimmering coals and finally expired entirely. When at last the chill of night crept through his bones, he stood with a creaking of joints and retired.

Waiting for them to arrive is going to be as hard as their journeys, no doubt.

Part II
Guide Us to Thy Perfect Light

At every crossroads on the path that leads to the future, tradition has placed 10,000 men to guard the past.

Maurice Maeterlinck

As has just been said: "Today, if you hear his voice, do not harden your hearts"

Hebrews, 3:15

Would you drop everything to follow a vision, a dream, a goal? If today a star appeared, would you gather your meager possessions and strike out on an unknown course to follow where it led?

Chapter 9
Gathering

Therefore, since we are surrounded by so great a cloud of witnesses, let us also lay aside every weight and sin, which clings so closely, and let us run with endurance the race that is set before us

Hebrews 12:1

As he pushed aside his evening cup of wine and crumb-littered plate, Balthazar leaned back and contemplated the swaying palm trees outside his dining area. The large trees looked at peace in their swaying. Buried in the gentle hush of the wind, he could hear the tranquil ripple of water in the gardens. He clenched his fists briefly as the memory of the beetles flickered through his mind. Then he rested his hands on the table and sighed. *Any day now, they should be—*

His chin shot up as his ears caught the familiar sound of hooves on the hard-packed ground. Leaping from his chair, he raced outside to see a rider approaching from the south, and a mile or so beyond him was another.

"They're here," he breathed.

Balthazar waved excitedly. His heart beat loudly in his chest and he felt as if he had run a thousand miles. Why? Was he sharing in their exertion or was something else going on?

Melchior returned the wave and shouted joyfully across the distance, though his voice was swallowed by the wind and the dust—this side of the palace sported only a couple of palm trees and faced the sprawling desert. The Nubian turned back as Jaspar's shout answered his and waved as fervently to the man who approached. Jaspar's camel shot forward and soon both men raced toward Balthazar, camels abreast of each other.

As Balthazar watched his friends approach, a wide smile broke across his face. Still, the strange feeling of nervousness that crawled up his spine was filtered with a great wave of sadness and joy at seeing his friends. He scampered out to greet them as they reared their camels to a stop.

The men dismounted hurriedly, each racing to meet Balthazar.

The three men greeted one another warmly, leaving their belongings on the animals. Dust flew into the hot air in great clouds as the friends embraced, the rough experiences all but forgotten in the pleasure of familiar company.

"I'm very glad to see each of you," Balthazar said after a few moments. "You have surely made a very rough journey here and I can't say how it pleases me that you're here." A glance at their haggard appearances betrayed a rough passage, though the two men did well to smile and push away the fatigue. Balthazar marked the emotion with a twinge—hosting their gathering, he felt guilty they had endured any hardship, yet beneath their warm exteriors, he could see shades of darkness and pain.

"Likewise," Melchior breathed. His face was caked with dust and sweat, puffy bags of skin drooped from exhausted eyes, and his dark complexion appeared a shade paler. The Nubian appeared to have aged several years. "It has been no easy journey, at least for me... How about you, Jaspar?" His words were only a fraction above a whisper.

"At one point I wasn't sure I'd survive!" He chuckled at that, but Balthazar saw dark clouds in his eyes. Jaspar's face was worn and slicked with grime. The King of Tharsis cracked a bent smile.

"I'm sorry it was so rough for you." Balthazar wanted to say more, to apologize, to offer anything to make it right, but held his tongue—this was a time for joy and celebration.

The King of Tharsis quickly recovered and nodded briskly. "We are here. That is all that matters. Now we are safe!"

Not safe from beetles. He scowled at the thought, then smiled back, hoping they missed his stumble. "Come!"

Balthazar ushered his friends to his palace, and his head servant darted outside to help with the belongings of the other rulers. As they each were shown to their quarters to freshen up from the ride, Balthazar wandered to the dining hall and waited for them, his mind again whirling with his previous thoughts. As he thought more about it, he realized the emotion had stemmed from the event with the beetles. Oddly, though, his mind kept trying to erase the horrible memory, and thinking on it took more and more effort. Perhaps he had learned his lesson, though he did not feel any wiser. The king had wandered through an entire day without a single thought of beetles—and Nador never made any mention of the event. He knocked his knuckles on the table. His friends had arrived; the time for dark thoughts and troubles was over.

The three kings sat around a low table in Balthazar's library, and a small fire burned in a soot-covered fireplace, taking the chill off the oncoming desert evening. Teapots and earthenware cups sat half-full on the table or were lifted to eager lips—weary from the soot and dust of travel, the hot liquid was soothing and uplifting.

Jaspar and Melchior had cleaned up well, the grime and dirt removed, and tired muscles had relaxed in nearly boiling baths. Oils and lotions were applied to weary faces, and dangerously thin bellies were filled with tea, water, and food. The food in Saba was much spicier than in either Tharsis or Nubia, but Melchior and Jaspar didn't seem to mind as they gobbled their pepper-laced dishes with abandon. Balthazar smiled, however, as ewers of water were refilled frequently.

"We should see quite a display of stars tonight, I think," Melchior said, setting down a teacup carefully in between two scrolls. It had been both a question and a statement; he was eager to scan the sky and hoping that clouds or thick humidity would not veil their view of the canopy.

"Yes, yes," Balthazar agreed. "Many stars we shall see." The image of the moving pile of beetles flashed in his mind, but faded as quickly as it came.

Jaspar silently sipped his tea.

"Yes, yes," Melchior aped Balthazar. "I didn't get much of a chance to look to the sky on my journey." He took a drink and glanced at Jaspar, who nodded agreement. "In any case, there is an idea in my head, an idea about the stars—but you know, it helps to actually see them!" He chuckled. His friends looked at him, faces calm and inviting, eyes wide and ears open, waiting for him to continue. He set his cup down and chewed his bottom lip briefly. "There is something I've been thinking about, and after reading many of the holy texts, I think my idea may have a foundation, but it may sound a little extreme—I thought about it during most of my journey northward."

"And what would that be, Melchior?" Balthazar asked softly.

"All of these stars... What if our own sun is such a star?"

At that, Jaspar sat upright. Such thinking could be dangerous, and he said as much. Men did not claim that the sun was not unique, that it was not the very center of the universe, the source and gift of life.

"He's right," Balthazar added, gesturing with a teacup. "According to many of the so-called 'learned,' the stars are merely holes of light within the firmament. To challenge that idea would be..." He trailed off, fingering his earlobe.

"But they *move!*" At that, he was greeted with wide stares from his companions. "No, no, not like planets." He shook his head. "It's just that certain constellations don't remain in the same position the whole year long—they shift. If they are just holes in the firmament, why and how could they move?" He paused and took in their expressions. Why were they so upset about this? What was so dangerous?

Jaspar leaned back in his chair and sighed softly. "He's right—I'm sure God would not punish us for trying to learn what the heavens do...," he said more to himself.

"Surely not... We are simply trying to understand His magnificence." Balthazar smiled briefly. *Who said anything about God being angry?* The situation seemed awkward to him, their companionship a little frayed; though they discussed their passion, the three rulers seemed nervous of one another, unsure. That would surely abate, the King of Saba hoped. The dust of the journey may be off their clothes, but not their minds yet. He feigned a yawn and added, "I hope God would be proud that we are trying to figure out His mysteries and the secrets of the stars."

Melchior leaned forward. "Exactly!"

The room seemed to lighten with his smile. Jaspar scowled briefly, then lit up. His shoulders seemed to lift; he drained his tea and set the cup down with a flourish.

Balthazar leaned back and smiled. "Melchior, you were saying...?" the King of Saba asked quietly, hands folded across his stomach.

"Yes, so... so what if..." He reached for an empty cup and spun it in his hands. "What if each one of those stars is a sun?" He set the cup down and leaned back, expecting more of a reaction than blank stares.

When neither companion said anything, he leaned forward again.

"My point is," he started, scratching his nose. The king let out a breath, careful to phrase his words wisely. He had been studying and thinking upon this for quite some time and did not want to sound arrogant and too self-assured. "Think of those countless stars that we see... so many that we can't even put a name to the number. What if some of those stars are suns like ours, and what if those suns, in turn, have worlds like ours that they illuminate?"

At that, the room fell deadly quiet. The only sound was a pop of gasses inside a burning ember.

"You mean...?" Balthazar began. He slowly unfolded his hands, leaned forward, and began to pour another cup of tea, but he set the pot down without dispensing a single drop.

"This challenges almost every religion," Jaspar said flatly.

"That's the thing," Melchior replied, veritably bouncing in his chair. He rubbed his hands together excitedly. "I'm not so sure that it does... After all, we only know this world. We only know the legends of God creating light, life, and the world. We only *know* this world," he repeated, as if confirming to himself. "So far, no one has come to tell us of others."

"Neither has God."

"But would He, Balthazar, *would* He? Even if He came down to our world? The line of thinking is very advanced, I agree, but what if it is true?"

"What of Mithra?" Jaspar wondered suddenly.

"Well... what of him? Many here in Saba follow his teachings and believe him some sort of, well—"

"Deity?" Jaspar answered for him. "You do realize he was heralded by a star?"

"It was a comet, actually," Balthazar corrected. *Where is this conversation going?* "But your point, I do see it clearly. Many feel that Mithra is god of the sun and, as such, is divine. Remember, though, that *god* is not *God*, in this sense. Divinity aside, he was not God come to earth, nor did he claim to be, as far as I know."

"Would God claim to be God, given what we have been discussing?" Melchior wondered.

Jaspar cleared his throat. "I question that as well."

"I don't think at first—I'm sure others would herald Him before. Perhaps one would come and anoint or baptize Him, or otherwise proclaim—"

"We come right back to the problem, then, don't we, Balthazar?"

Balthazar sighed. "Yes, we do. That even such a person places himself in danger. To state that a man—a living man—is God? No, such a claim puts your neck out for the scimitar. But surely, *surely*, if God wanted man to believe, He would inspire them, maybe with a sign, a voice, clouds—who knows? Maybe a comet or another moon, or—"

"A star," Jaspar breathed. "Yes, you come right back to where you have started. And the question remains, why were none of the other divines truly God come to earth?"

"You think they, perhaps, were God come to earth?"

"No, Balthazar, I don't know what to think. Melchior's point is valid—we only know that *we don't know.* Do you think you can understand the mind of God?"

Balthazar rubbed his earlobe furiously, dropped his hand into his lap, then threw up both hands in the air, his right fist balled briefly, then unclenched. "I don't know the mind of God, either, Melchior, nor do I—I'm sorry," he said at last, shaking his head. He was about to say *nor do I intend to.*

Thankfully, his friend did not take offense at the comment and continued his line of discourse. "I'm not saying you do. It is late; our tongues are heavy and eyes even more so. I just wonder what it would be like if God were to come to earth, or to another one of the planets that has life... What would people do?"

"I assume you mean for us to ignore the possibility that Mithra, and others, were *not* true deities?"

"Of course. What would it be like? How would people react?"

Balthazar's eyes were sad as he looked up, the orange light of the fire reflected off them in odd dancing shapes. "They would kill him."

It was Melchior's first instinct to protest, but he bit his lower lip and thought for a moment. "Why do you say that?" he asked softly.

"Throughout the ages, countless false prophets and false messiahs have been strung up, or worse. Each man or woman who has claimed to be the chosen one, the son of God, or even God Himself, are dragged off to their deaths. It is the way of humans." He paused, sighed loudly. "We wait patiently for the coming of God, and yet when those of us claim to be God, we kill them."

"But surely those pretenders were just that," Melchior said, gesturing with his hands palms up. "They could perform no miracles, could not prove they were of God."

"That much is true, but how do you think God would react, knowing the fate of those who set themselves up as false deities?"

Melchior bit his lip. "I'm afraid you are correct. He would know this, and know the hearts of men—that no matter who believed, and who followed, many would see them as false and have them removed..." It was Melchior's turn to sigh. "They would never believe who He was, regardless of the signs he gave. I know you said that earlier, that He would have to do something to show the world that He had come... Nothing short of 'This is my incarnation, and I am well pleased with Him,' would work!"

Balthazar nodded.

"But even if He could somehow convert the minds of men to convince them that he were there—" Jaspar cracked a knuckle.

"Such an action would be beneath Him, I think."

"How so, Balthazar?" Melchior wondered.

"Well..." the King of Saba started, his thumb hovering close to his earlobe. "The God I believe in doesn't need to warp or bend men to his will—He does not have to cloud minds, create false visions, or any of that. Men are expected to take Him for what He is."

"And what is He?"

Balthazar had no answer to Melchior's question, and Jaspar continued to stare into the flames, thinking. Absently, the king of Tharsis stood and tossed another small log onto the fire, and at once, the room was filled with the sweet and ancient smell of incense. The servants had recently trimmed a few long-deceased branches of the boswellia trees and stacked a nice pile in the library. As the log burned, it gave off little smoke, but intense heat as the petrified resins inside of it burned slowly. The smell gave off only a hundredth of the cloying aroma that newer trees possessed, but enough fragrance to offer a gentle and soothing backdrop to their conversation.

"I know, I know," Melchior said after a moment's silence, watching as the log burned. "We can't know the mind of God, but the question is still there. What would God do if He came down, and what would it take for men not to murder him when He did so?"

"A thousand more years," the King of Saba replied sadly.

There was a long silence as the men stared into the fire.

"If God came to earth, that would still be a spectacular thing." Jaspar's voice was soft and measured, but it rang as loud as a summoning bell. He had been silent for most of the conversation, and at the sound of his voice, the others looked up abruptly.

"So many prophecies speak of it, talk as if it were a sure thing. As if it is bound to happen... Spectacular indeed, but not out of the realm of possibility," Melchior stated.

Jaspar sighed. "That is all well and good. Do you think we would ever see something like that in our lifetime?"

"It would be miraculous," Balthazar said, glancing outside briefly. "Miraculous indeed."

"So God created all of these worlds... these worlds that might exist?" Jaspar asked.

Melchior looked confused for a second. His mind had been firmly attached to their recent discussion, and the swift change to the previous topic seemed sudden. He looked at Balthazar, who shared his look, but quickly recovered his bearings and asked simply, "Why not?"

"And how would He possibly visit everyone? On all worlds?"

"He's God, Jaspar. Does it warrant more of an answer?" He stopped suddenly and rubbed his temples. "I'm sorry, I didn't mean to sound—"

Jaspar waved him off. "Not to worry."

"We can't understand the ways of God," Balthazar said. "But I do think, that if there were all of these worlds created by Him, He would have no trouble visiting them. No trouble inspiring men's minds to do what is right and good."

Melchior poured some tea and leaned back in his chair, sipping thoughtfully. "There's a difference between inspiring and coercing, though... but the line is a fine one."

"It is very difficult to try to know when God is willing something and when man is willing something," Jaspar replied. "I often wonder when it is my will or someone else's, or what the greater good of the people will be. Whenever I hear an advisor tell me God wants me to do something, I question deeply whether it is truly God's will, or the advisor's. It's always—"

"Your advisor's, I know," Balthazar said, nodding. "It is often that way here as well."

"But God would not coerce. That is my real point."

"Agreed, Melchior, agreed." Balthazar stood and tossed another small log onto the fire.

Soon their conversation switched from deeper mysteries to the patterns of the stars and the various names their people had for the constellations. Surprisingly, their cultures were very close in how stars were used for navigation, and even the names of the constellations. The three kings also discussed distances, time, and the possibility of other earth-like planets. Teapots were refreshed, and larger logs tossed onto the fire as the night wore slowly on.

It was nearly dawn by the time they dragged their exhausted bodies to their sleeping quarters.

Chapter 10
A Star

Before I formed you in the womb I knew you, and before you were born I
consecrated you; I appointed you a prophet to the nations.
Jeremiah 1:5

It was well past the setting of the sun of the following day, past the rising and setting of the moon, and nearer to dawn when Jaspar stood with a yawn. For a second night, the three kings had immersed themselves in intense discussions. The gilded table before them was littered with scrolls, teacups, and crumbs from a half-eaten spice cake. The three leaders of strange lands had been gazing at the stars, returning to the scrolls, and talking about past and future events. Melchior was passionate about his thoughts on the panorama of stars and the possibility of other life forms, but the thought of billions and *billions* of stars, other planets, and the possibility of life on those planets was enough to set Jaspar's head pounding. Such large numbers were unheard of, and they struggled to find words even to describe multiples of millions of stars. Jaspar rose and went to the balcony to stare, not at the canopy of stars, but at the ornate gardens.

His focus had been drawn to the heavens for so long that the gardens were a refreshing diversion. The trees, hedges, trellises, and gentle water were nearer to his soul and relaxing. Stars would draw his heart and mind, but the tangible enjoyments of the world were not to be missed, either. Compared to the desolation of Tharsis, the network of green growth was like a morsel of fruit after a long fast—one felt slightly satiated, but still hungry for a deeper forest, a large meal of green foliage and cool water.

The water in the irrigation channels barely reflected the wan starlight, and speckles danced upon tiny waves born on a very slight wind. In the purplish hue of the water, he could see reflections of the darker green gardens and the incense trees. For some time he stared and had nearly turned around to return inside when a brighter flicker caught his attention. He would have missed it had a gust of wind not pushed a wave across a wading pool; a flash of pure-white light was reflected off the rise in water, and only the very corner of Jaspar's eye caught it. First, he looked to the water, then shunned himself for a fool, quickly darting his gaze to the sky.

There, to the west, seemingly only a hundred paces from the edge of the earth, a star illuminated the land. A star he had never before seen, never catalogued, and he had spent countless nights watching the sky twist and turn above him. This new star was far larger than any in the sky, larger than should be possible, and it looked as if it were only hundreds of feet above the earth instead of millions of miles away like the others. He rubbed his eyes to erase what was surely a strange vision, but when he looked again, the star was still there. It seemed to pulsate with white light, and as it did, it took on the shape of a cross—*A cross? Where have I seen a cross before?* The shape of the orb and its overflowing brightness seemed at once familiar and foreign to him. Jaspar knew he had seen such a thing before, but where?

The scrolls! Surely, something must be within the huge pile of papers. He stumbled backward into the apartments, eyes locked on the glowing orb, his feet clumsy and unsteady.

Just yesterday, they had been discussing a few ancient prophecies, and one had mentioned a star; the translations were so varied that the meaning of that star was muddled and confused, and they had quickly moved on to other subjects. *But what were they talking about?*

he wondered as he fell back into the room. His mind was locked so tightly upon the image, his eyes burning with the brightness, that his mind felt completely empty of anything his companions had been discussing.

He turned to face the room and stopped, staring at his sandals. The change of scenery had snapped his attention back to prior discussions and freed him slightly from the pull of the star. *Yes,* he thought, *a star, mentioned several times, in several languages.* There were prophecies surrounding stars, but also many simple phrases and meanings. It could mean a range of things, from an oncoming rainstorm to the descent of God to earth. But no matter the interpretation, the star meant something good—not even a word remotely related to negativity was to be had in those scrolls. Still, it didn't hurt to ask. Perhaps there was something he had forgotten.

"Do either of you remember anything about a star shaped like a cross?" he asked breathlessly. His companions had watched him stumble into the room as if intoxicated, and now, they almost gawked at him, mouths open, teacups held in mid-air, eyes washed with concern.

"There—there are lots of stories about that," Melchior said, leaning slightly forward. He stifled a yawn, though the concern did not fade from his face. "Why, why do you ask?"

"Well, what do those stories discuss?" The words sounded clipped, demanding, sharp, though he was trying to rein himself in.

Melchior seemed not to notice. "It's usually something beneficial, or prophesizing the birth of a new child, a new sheep, the death of an evil man, the coming of rains for crops to grow." He looked into his teacup, brought it toward his lips, then set it down, untouched. "The list goes on and on. Why?"

"Well, I..." He wrung his hands and cast a nervous glance over his shoulder. "I, er..."

"What is it?" Balthazar asked.

"I think you both had better come out here and look," he said, his voice hoarse. He could have easily thrown back the curtain over the open transom, but feared the others would not see; after all, they could not see the glow through the doorframe that led outside. He wrung his hands again as they extracted themselves from their couches and trundled outside. When Balthazar and Melchior looked out above the gardens, their mouths hung agape.

"It's..." Balthazar started. "I... This star, we all see it, correct?" he asked, turning to face his companions. The light of the star reflected off his sun-bronzed features and the pools of his eyes glowed in the radiant light.

"We all see it," Jaspar whispered. His dark eyes twinkled. Framed in the brilliant light, he looked stoically majestic, fully like the king he was.

"I think it moved!"

"No, Melchior," Balthazar reproached him softly, "stars don't move. Planets and comets, now they do, but stars—" He stopped suddenly.

The star *had* moved. It seemed to *bounce* slightly farther to the west, and then back eastward. As it did so, it glowed with a slight pulsing, its pointed edges solid, but yet there was an appearance of motion. It looked as if it were daring them to follow, its glowing aura lending the impression of an animal urging the humans to follow it.

"I saw it move. It wants something..." Melchior breathed. "Wait, I have an idea!" Like a giddy child, he hopped on his sandals, then raced down the stone staircase, leaping two at a time. His garments fluttered behind him as he sprinted along the walkways in the gardens. As he neared the tree-lined edge of the sprawling gardens, the star did indeed bounce farther to the west. With a harrumph, he picked his way through the trees and out into the scrub-covered field beyond.

The star moved east.

"Aha!" he exclaimed, returning to the palace. As he cast a glance over his shoulder, he saw the star had moved *closer* to him, and then bounced again a few hundred paces to the west. "You want us to follow you?" he asked. The star dipped slightly.

"It wants us to follow it, does it?" Balthazar asked. "If we didn't all see this thing, I'd think we'd been up too late and our minds had faded. We *have* been up too late!" He smiled, but an edge of concern seemed to drift into his tone. "Hmm, very interesting, that. What do you say we should do?"

"We follow," Melchior and Jaspar said simultaneously, then looked at each other with wide eyes.

"I see." Balthazar thumbed his earlobe and stared at the patterned mosaic on the floor.

"Wait! I'm not so sure where that came from, why I said that... I—"

Melchior turned to face Jaspar. "I know it sounds odd, and we have had little sleep, at least you and I—"

"I've slept very little awaiting your arrival," Balthazar interjected. He shivered, thinking back on his encounter with the beetles. Though the starlight showed dark circles under their eyes, each man's face looked younger and more vibrant; the strain and trial of their journey looked to be washed away.

"Exactly. So, yes, Jaspar, this does seem strange and odd, and marvelous all at once. But something prompted us to answer as one. It's the same something that no doubt kept us alive on our journey here, or—"

"Or caused my feeling of mourning..."

"Feeling of mourning, Jaspar?" Balthazar wondered.

"Yes, why? Did you feel it too?"

"Indeed," he responded, thumbing his ear. "I could not put a name to it—but I felt it as you two were riding up to the palace. It felt as if someone were about to die, and that someone was me!"

Jaspar sucked in air and looked at the star. Its long tail looked like a sword, pointing sharply to Earth, while its gently pulsating upper reaches seemed to be pulling light down from some unseen source as its glow intensified. At its nucleus, where the bars of the cross met, light swirled slowly, from left to right; eventually, tendrils of radiating white light suddenly spun away from the center, creating circles within circles.

"Look!" Melchior said. "It is changing again... thirteen," he whispered. Indeed, the number of circles was thirteen. Then suddenly they coalesced into a definite shape, a luminous rosette, a braid of perfect light formed in the hub of the star.

"Birth, death... rebirth," Balthazar breathed, staring at the glowing shape.

"Death," Jaspar repeated.

"Our deaths." Melchior chewed his lip and turned his focus away from the star, instead looking at its wobbling reflection in the numerous pools of light.

For nearly five minutes, the men stared at the star, and slowly, the rosette uncurled itself and the hub of the star returned to its previous state. Again, there was a slight bob to the west, followed by a dimming of the light.

After a moment, Jaspar nodded slowly, then turned to face his companions. "The rosette—birth, death, rebirth." He heaved a heavy sigh. "As soon as I left that small mountain range and started north, I felt it. At first, I thought I was just nervous about our meeting and about all the things we were going to discuss, but the more I dwelt upon it, I realized that I was mourning my own death."

Melchior's face turned ashen. "Death?" he whispered. The King of Tharsis had said the word as if he were announcing the arrival of a tray of sweets. Surely, it was just the excitement... death. *Death?*

"Not like that," Jaspar said hurriedly.

"I know what you mean, I think," Melchior responded in a hoarse voice. *At least, I would like to believe.* "Not true death, but a passing-away nonetheless."

"Something of ourselves will die should we follow the star," Jaspar repeated. "Perhaps we will be reborn, but how?"

Balthazar shook his head and his gaze locked upon the star. It appeared he had not been listening. "So what does it mean? Is this star the source of our previous feelings?"

"We think it is our deaths," Melchior repeated for him. It was understandable that Balthazar had not been paying attention. The star seemed to pull all attention toward itself. "And, yes, if we are expected to follow, then we may have found the source of our earlier feelings. Mourning, loss, sadness—it makes some sense." Melchior paused. "Perhaps it is leading us somewhere important, or to somebody important."

"But why?" Jaspar wondered. "We are men who study the stars and the planets. What would we need to discover here on Earth?"

"That is a good question, but perhaps you have already answered it," Balthazar replied.

"How so?"

The king shrugged. "We have been gazing at the stars all these years, and surely since we were in the cradle. This—this is all we know. If the stars have led us to the Earth, or at least something on Earth, surely it is a great change for us."

"A dying of our old selves," Jaspar whispered.

"Indeed." Balthazar's hand floated instinctively toward his ear, but he let it drop atop the gilded railing and stared out at the sparkling gardens. "Indeed," he repeated.

"There must be something in store for us should we choose to follow." Jaspar breathed in and then added hastily, "Nothing of material value."

"I don't think it is limited to just ourselves, Melchior," Balthazar answered. "We cannot be the only ones who see this; we should go back through the history and the prophecies with care. After looking at this now, I think there is something buried that we are forgetting."

"Perhaps another race has come from one of those planets?" Jaspar asked.

"It could be that, but it is most likely nearer to the subject you had been discussing earlier."

"You don't mean... Balthazar, that would be quite the coincidence!" Melchior exclaimed.

"This is not a coincidence." The ruler of Saba smiled.

"Why would you say that?" Jaspar asked.

"Surely we have each felt our own fading from this world, our own deaths, as you put it. We've come together under difficult circumstances and across dangerous ground. You both have, though I'm sure my trials are only beginning, but could that star not be our sign? We have seen how it waits for us and jumps to the west, begging us to follow it. How can that not be God?"

"God?" Jaspar wondered.

"God," Balthazar repeated.

Melchior sucked in air and bit his lower lip. "But nothing like this happened on our first, or even second, meeting! I would love nothing more than to believe that it is so!"

"Your first instinct was correct, certainly," Jaspar said, his voice low and soft, deep and rich. "Our first instinct, that is. Trust it. Let us all trust it and go on our journey. The feelings we had on our trek here were indeed feelings of mourning; as I thought to myself, I realized the ruler of Tharsis was no more, and in his place was a new man. This"—he pointed to the star—"is our sign. No matter that we were just discussing it. In the fullness of time, surely it is possible that we would be witnesses to God's presence on Earth!"

Melchior nodded.

"And," Balthazar put in, "although I believe God does not coerce or cloud our minds, I do believe He lights fires. He plants sparks of thought and seeds of understanding. Especially on this night, I do believe in that. We had been marveling over how it would be should He come down to Earth… and now…" He, too, pointed at the star. All eyes returned to the glowing orb.

"It is still very convenient," Melchior said. "We've just been discussing God, stars and comets, Mithras and his status as a deity and now—now God just drops down and greets us?" He bit his lower lip.

"Melchior, your pessimism, it is sometimes misplaced."

"It's not pessimism, Balthazar. I only feel this is too close of a coincidence."

"Too close?" Jaspar inquired. Melchior nodded. "Hmm, perhaps you feel it is not God, but something worse?"

Balthazar's mouth worked; words eventually tumbled out awkwardly. "From my conversation earlier, I would hope you had learned that God would inspire, not coerce."

"But the star—the star moves!"

"Yes, Melchior, yes. It moves, but nothing else."

"What do you mean?"

Jaspar cracked his knuckles. "He means, Melchior, that the star is not reaching out and pulling you toward it. It simply bounces and waits. Waits for us to follow. I would not doubt if it were God out there."

"But what if it is *not* God out there?" The question now seemed hollow and vain. He was prone to doubt, true, but there was doubting and being a complete boor.

"Melchior, my dear friend, if it is not God Himself out there, it may well be Him leading us somewhere."

"Then we follow," Jaspar said softly. "We follow," he repeated, looking into Melchior's eyes.

The Nubian shrugged. "We follow."

"We follow," Balthazar said, adding the third affirmation to their journey. As soon as the words flitted from his lips, the fire flared, having caught a particularly flammable section of resin. Coupled with the star's illumination, the bright light of the fire cast a vivid glow over the three rulers; for a moment they looked cast in gold.

"What if... what if it *isn't* something from God?" The voice of Melchior was only a whisper, but in the dead silence of the night, it sounded like a shout.

"No."

"Balthazar, how can you be sure? What if—?"

"No," the King of Saba repeated sternly. "The devil can be cunning indeed, and surely we have been tricked a time or two in our lives. But always there is a feeling that goes with such cunning, a slimy feeling on your soul, a little voice that tells you what you are doing is wrong. I feel none of that. Do either of you?"

The men shook their heads slowly.

"Then we can forget that line of thought. Until we're given more evidence that we follow something...

unholy... we'll continue. It's late and we're tired. Your concerns are real, but we can't keep second-guessing ourselves, either."

Melchior nodded.

"Well, then," Balthazar sighed. "I will need to recall my servants and retainers... in case we find ourselves traveling a great distance. The ancient prophecies seemed to be coming true, no matter the source, and if it's God..." He trailed off, thumbing his earlobe.

In the late-night excitement over the phenomenon, following the glowing orb seemed the most logical and correct thing to do. None of the men questioned; none of the men doubted they should go. Something seemed to be tugging at their hearts, their minds, and most of all, their legs—a gentle push that nudged them to where the sun set each day.

$

Before retiring, Balthazar proceeded to Nador's chambers and gently woke him. "Nador... Nador, wake up. I have a task for you." The man did not stir. He moved to poke him again, when images of his childhood flashed through his mind's eye.

He could see his younger self, enjoying the constant companionship of his lead servant. Nador, the scruffy, always-smiling man who was always hovering over Balthazar, watching him. Protecting him. They would play games in the gardens, games of find-me-if-you-can, and every so often Balthazar and Nador would play together against other servants. In so doing, they developed signals only they shared, mainly of birds or other animals of Saba.

Balthazar tapped him gently once more and repeated his call, and finally, Nador stirred; the servant groaned again and rolled on his back, and for a moment, Balthazar considered using one of those signals, but already lids were fluttering open. "W-what is it, Majesty? I—wait, did you just call me...?" His brain was slowly processing Balthazar's words.

"I did and from now on, you can call me Balthazar. Don't look at me like that. No, the revolution has not started. We're going on a journey... Melchior, Jaspar, and I, and we'll need help."

"H-how long of a—" He cracked a massive yawn. "How long, Your M—how long?" he asked again. While in their youth, Balthazar had called him by name, but Nador was forbidden to do likewise, though they were fast friends—using the first name of his king was nearly impossible for him.

"We're not sure. We are following a sign in the sky."

"I will get the others and be back in the morning," Nador said flatly, swinging his legs down from his bed. He yawned again.

"Thank you."

Balthazar at once embraced this devotion, and at once shied from it—such loyalty could be dangerous. One needed a companion who would question motives and decisions, and not merely accept orders as given. Then again, Balthazar mused, Nador's actions were not blind—since his king was a man of the stars, it would stand to reason he'd wander off and chase one at some point. At that he laughed.

"What is it, Your Majesty?"

For now, Balthazar ignored the formality. "You are a dear man, Nador. Many others would laugh in my face, even with my crown! We're going to follow a star. A star! And yet you nod and follow."

Nador looked at him, his face sincere. "Pardon me, Your Maj—pardon me, but what else would I do?"

§

Sleepy servants and retainers arrived in the pre-dawn hours, yawning and stretching aching muscles from their hurried summons. Many tended to camels and a few horses, while others got to work packing carts, saddle bags, and food stores. Nador dashed about the palace, organizing the effort to the best of his ability—he was dead-tired and the comforts of sleep seemed as if they would be unreachable. Balthazar had ordered him to work no longer than a few hours and return to his bed, but there was too much to do.

The servants had assumed the rulers were visiting some foreign dignitary, and thus packed far more than was necessary or reasonable. Nador found himself removing silver and golden goblets, plates from trunks, untying frilly shawls from camels, and unpacking heavy boxes of expensive tea and tobacco. If Balthazar were following a star, there was no need for this excess. Instead, he organized a more productive system of packing.

Only foods in jars or dried foods were packed in the cart pulled by the strongest mule. Water was poured into skins and added to this, the heaviest cart. Thick blankets were folded compactly and packed away, while pillows and sheets were left aside. Nador allowed only a few logs and fire-making supplies to be added to the bottom of a cart where he placed medicinal herbs, poultices, and tonics. The vast number of scrolls were light and placed on the weakest animal. When he finished his work, Nador stepped back to marvel at the caravan he had assembled: a dozen camels, mules, and several more carts and large shoulder-carried packs arrayed in the courtyard. And next to the assembled gear was a monstrous pile of unnecessary, frivolous items, which he ordered returned to the main hall—it could be sorted when they returned.

Exhausted, he bade the others to rest until sundown of the next day. Every person would need as much rest as they could muster. Nador marveled at their dedication, even in the middle of the night. Each man and woman seemed as driven as the kings to travel to their as-yet-unknown destination, and oddly enough, not a soul complained or uttered begrudging remarks about their tasks—filling a supply caravan to travel several thousand miles once, and then emptying them and starting over upon Nador's orders. *That,* he thought, *is true dedication.*

On his way back to his quarters, he paused to chat with a friend.

"They are chasing a star, huh?"

"Yes, a very bright one indeed. It—" He paused and looked to the west, where Balthazar had said the star was. "It's over there, I guess. Can't miss it."

"I don't see anything."

Nador looked and shook his head. "I don't see it, either, but it must have been a bright moon for us to work by or it's gone with the coming daylight. Did you notice how bright it was?"

"It was bright enough to work by, but I didn't look up!" He gave Nador a look that said, *You were pushing us so hard.*

"I wonder if anyone else saw the star?"

The other man shook his head roughly and coughed. "Ach, get some sleep, Nador… Who knows how far we will go?"

How far indeed, Nador thought. "I think quite far," he answered, but the man had already vanished.

$

When the sun fell off the horizon, Melchior arose and sought the star, though a small part of him hoped it was not there—that they had dreamed the entire episode, or had consumed a batch of spoiled tea and their minds had been damaged. To both his elation and his dismay, he could make out a light glimmer in the fading blue of twilight that was barely visible, but grew stronger as the void of night slowly swallowed the brightness of the day.

"God help us," he whispered, watching as the orb's brightness increased. He yawned and then chewed his lip. *I had better wake the others, though Balthazar is probably already about.*

The Nubian trudged down the corridors and woke his companions. It had not been terribly difficult to sleep during the day, having been awake all night—even Balthazar snored loudly when Melchior approached. Yet, as the kings arose and moved about, the prolonged time abed had made them feel less refreshed and slightly more lethargic. They dined in relative silence before trudging to their camels.

Jaspar gasped at the sight of their procession, lined up on the western edge of the sprawling gardens. Nearly twenty servants tended the animals Nador had arranged, some riding them, some leading, and others carrying the tall packs on their backs. Having traveled so lightly on the way to Saba, he felt like an entire empire waited to travel with them.

Melchior's gold was secured in a dirty cart, while the myrrh and incense were piled on another to conceal the richness of the cargo. The size of their traveling group would provide some deterrence for bandits, but the threat was real, so a weapon or two were stashed within the carts. Nador had thought of this at the last minute and told nobody, least of all the rulers—they would have surely had him dispose of such implements.

A few more orders were given, straps tightened, animals patted, and carts checked, before the long train eased its way westward; for now, Balthazar and his friends rode at the vanguard, eyes locked on their guide.

Nador rode his camel up and down the line, chatting with the servants, double- and triple-checking everything. When he mentioned the phenomenon of the glowing orb, not a single servant acknowledged they could see the star.

Chapter 11
Over Field and Fountain

A voice cries: In the wilderness prepare the way of the Lord; make straight in the desert a highway for our God.
Isaiah 40:3

The purple dark of night, pocked with stars and the steam of traveling men and beasts, could barely hide the barren, dusty desert. The three kings were used to the climate, the sunbaked rock, scorched dust, and jagged gravel, but the desolation was so extreme that it was hopeless. At one point, Balthazar called the terrain a field, surely in jest, but the joke faded with his cold breath in the night—all eyes remained locked upon the star, only darting away to check the footing of the beasts.

Several times Nador rode to the front of the line, insisting he take the lead, though he admitted that he could not see the star. Balthazar respectfully heard the concerns of his servant, appreciated Nador's wish for his ruler's safety, and sternly sent him back to the other retainers.

The men trotted in silence for several long and dark hours. Melchior opened his mouth to speak on several occasions, but clasped his lips shut, choosing instead to gnaw on them quietly. Ahead of them, the star pulsed its perfect, pure radiance; the Nubian time and again worked his mind over the power and wonder of the star, and the God behind its light. *It has to be God. It just must to be,* he reminded himself. But to his horror, there was still a nagging doubt, a fear that they chased something else. Could the Devil be so deceiving? Or would God be selective in whom He sought to follow?

Why did the servants not see it?

Why? he thought, ears ringing from the shout echoing in his head.

He bore down on his chapped lips and scowled at the star, though an emotion somewhere on the border between peace and resignation settled in his heart and the scowl vanished, replaced by a thin line of set lips. The star had no answers, surely, but Melchior thought he heard a whisper, rather felt it, shot forth from the glowing body—a reassurance, a hope of comfort. It was weak, but he could feel it. Or was it just another deception?

Melchior kept his doubts to himself and smiled freely, while Balthazar seemed unable to tear his gaze away from the beacon. Jaspar looked back and forth between his friends as he talked, giving each full attention as they chatted idly.

On a night when the stars were blurred by a rare bank of high clouds, Nador bounded forth with at least one more stern objection, before Balthazar kindly reprised him and sent him back to the line. The man was hard to convince, for he had served his king nearly the entirety of his life, and watching his ruler in the lead set his nerves on edge. But Balthazar was persistent and, finally, Nador grudgingly returned to the retinue. Even through the wisps of clouds, rare as they were in this climate, the star glimmered and capered to the west.

They traveled along a vast and barren desert, the ground a hard-packed clay with stretches of rough, sliding gravel every few miles. The animals struggled to push through the slag and their handlers whispered and cooed them on. The kings followed the star, riding three camels on the hard ground and walking them in the gravel. A moon was out, but not enough light filtered down to the earth to illuminate smaller obstructions or depressions in the ground, and a servant or two found themselves fumbling for purchase. Strangely, even those exhausted from sleep deprivation carried forward, a phenomenon the three kings hoped would continue. Several days had already passed and the initial rush of excitement had faded into a steady, determined march forward.

$

A few nights passed quietly, pocked with idle chatter. Melchior kept his doubts to himself and smiled freely, while Balthazar seemed unable to tear his gaze away from their beacon. Jaspar looked back and forth between his friends as he talked, giving each full attention as they chatted idly. On one cold evening, the stars were blurred by a rare bank of high clouds, but even through the wispy of veil, the star glimmered and capered to the west.

For the travelers, three kings included, the adjustment to night travel and daytime rest was a hard one. Several found themselves unable to sleep during the day, even in tents drawn over with opaque cloth. These men and women could be identified by their drawn faces and deep circles beneath their eyes; while they did their best to carry their burden, the loss of sleep took much from them. It would take several nights of traveling to adjust to the reversed schedule.

The animals struggled to push through the hard-packed clay, and their handlers whispered and cooed them into pushing through. Strangely, even those exhausted from sleep deprivation carried forward, a phenomenon that the three kings hoped would continue... several days had already passed and the initial rush of excitement had faded into a steady, determined march forward.

$$\phi$$

During the next evening's journey, the landscape changed slightly. The hard-packed earth was replaced entirely by gravel, which slowed down the animals considerably. Small stones would often poke into the hooves of camels and mules, some sharp enough that the beasts would rear in agony; their huge bodies were cajoled and caressed as the objects were removed.

Several painfully slow hours passed before the travelers found themselves on a hard-packed trail that wound through the coarse shingle. The winding channel, however, looked more like an accident of geology than any set path.

As the small, gravel track advanced into higher elevation, the pebbles gave way to sand and then weed-splattered rock; the star still shone brightly ahead of them, and a large moon illuminated the trail clearly. Even as the trail bent and dipped along irregular ground, the star followed its motions, proceeding ever westward.

When they took a break near dawn, Melchior looked back to the south and east, along the ridge of the plateau. Then his breath caught as he opened his viewing field to assess the expanse of wilderness below.

A breathtaking, dizzying landscape spanned majestically in the distance; the earth was as barren as Balthazar's "field," but reflected in the wan glow of the oncoming dawn, it was gorgeous. Immense pillars of stone rose from the rock, their upper reaches glowing red with the morning rays of the sun, their tops flat. Dried streambeds skittered across the surface of the land, dotted now and again with tiny, prickly scrub and small piles of rock. Melchior's jaw hung loose—it looked as if the landscape went on forever, the huge pillars dotting the land for endless miles, smaller boulders like grains of sand towered beneath them, and the whitewashed riverbeds painted the acreage in a rich fabric of creation.

Tears welled in the Nubian's eyes as he turned back to his companions. *Perhaps there is something to be found on this journey.*

"What is it, Melchior?" Balthazar wondered.

Silently, he walked to his tent and paused, a hand on the flap. "God is great," he said softly before ducking inside.

$

After sunset, and a restless day of sleep, the men supped and packed their gear, but not before taking extended, longing looks down at the panorama. The trail angled away from the plateau sharply and the star still hung high above the pathway—as the collection of men and women struck out toward the star, the path again became dull, the landscape monotonous, and the three kings were soon lolling in their saddles.

"What is that?" Melchior wondered aloud, his own eyes heavy as they struggled to open against the force of exhaustion.

"Fire...," Jaspar whispered.

A pillar of flame jetted out from an oval fissure in the gravel. A ring of knee-high rocks around the opening gave it the appearance of a fountain, though instead of a constant stream of clean water, gouts of flame boiled from its source. A thick black smoke coiled violently into the chill night air, and tendrils of yellow-orange fire dripped from the bursting cascade of flame, rolling from the main source in small waves. It was an exact duplicate of a city fountain. A heavy, fetid smell wafted to the observers as the flames curled in their direction, the smell of ancient lamp oil, rancid and moldy with time.

The heat of the fountain overpowered the cold desert night in its immediate area. It billowed out almost visibly; its shimmering and wobbling aura flowed from the towering fountain of flame in waves, glowing against the chilled barrier beyond. Sweat glistened on the travelers' faces, but as soon as a tuft of cold desert air wafted in from another direction, the sweat turned cold and clammy. As the three kings neared the fire, its heat quickly overpowered any cold bursts of air.

"What fuel would there be for a fire?" Jaspar asked.

Balthazar did not hear the question over the dull roar of the flame. He had pulled his camel to a stop and dismounted. "I've heard of these strange things before…," he muttered. To his companions' surprise, he started walking toward the glowing flame. "Don't worry," he called over his shoulder. "It's harmless."

"But…" Melchior started, then dismounted with a grunt. "Fire," he muttered to himself, "burning without wood… quite harmless?" *This is dangerous. What has the star led us to? He's going to walk into the fire, and—*

As if he had heard, Balthazar stopped and pointed to the glowing flame. "Come, but don't get too close. It *is* harmless. Fuel, it does consume."

Jaspar had dismounted and started walking toward Melchior. He muttered as he walked past the stationary king to look over Balthazar's shoulder. The sound of their sandaled feet on gravel was drowned by the dull purr of fire.

Their faces were soon covered in a thick sheen of sweat, while the cool air chilled their backs. Jaspar wasn't sure if he should shiver or shed his robe. "What feeds the fire?"

"Oil," Balthazar said flatly, answering Jaspar with a sidelong glance. "Oil or sometimes a gas—"

"Gas? What do you mean?" Melchior wondered.

"Here, in the desert, a very flammable gas runs deep below, along with thick oil. It—the oil—does not always come to the top, but when it does, it can burn like this." He balled his fists briefly, then nodded. "I've seen such fountains before. Some give off a smell, and others don't. Father said the ones that gave off no smell burned only gas, since gas wouldn't have any impurities. I never understood how he knew that, but he knew many things." The ruler of Saba fingered his earlobe and his eyes narrowed, then moistened. He wiped them with the backs of his fingers.

"What kind of oil? As in a lamp?" Melchior wondered, scratching his head. *Oil and gas beneath the earth?*

"In a way, but thicker and darker. Do you see the thick smoke? The oil is deep beneath the earth, and sometimes it bubbles up."

"But," Jaspar wondered, "how does it catch fire?"

"There are storms here, sometimes—maybe once per seven years. Maybe embers from another fire that are brought by the wind." Balthazar stared into the roiling flames and turned away. "Well of Fire," he breathed. "Father called these Wells of Fire. Some people even—"

He broke off as several of the serving men and women rushed up to the edge of the fountain and knelt in the gravel. Lips moved in silent prayer and wide-open eyes reflected the flickering light. Their exhausted faces looked reborn and refreshed as the bright light washed them.

"Worship the fire," Balthazar whispered, finishing his thought. "Some people intentionally light the oil wells that bubble up."

After several minutes of prayer, the servants arose and walked past the kings, their heads lowered. The last man to pass whispered something in Balthazar's ear before scurrying back to the caravan.

"What did he say?" Jaspar wondered.

"He merely said that these wells of fire are a sign of greatness and a sign of trouble. He admonished me to be careful. Fire can purify and it can destroy."

"So they do worship the fire?"

"They have been called the Fire Worshippers in other kingdoms, that is true. But in Saba, there are very few." He stopped and looked back at the line of servants. "Well, perhaps more than I thought." He pinched his earlobe briefly. "Often they are accused of worshipping fire over God, or gods, depending on the sect, but they will tell you they only worship God. The fire is their path to their God—the healing and the hurting, the pain and the joy."

"Fire can also symbolize the Devil," Jaspar said carefully, looking back quickly at the servants. "Can it not?"

"It can and does," Balthazar said. "According to some... but these worshippers, the Devil—the Devil, they do not worship."

"I—" Melchior began and broke off. *How can you be so sure?* A bright flash behind them forced their attention back to the west, breaking the Nubian's bleak thought.

The star hung motionless in the sky.

"What...?"

"Jaspar, we should continue," Balthazar said softly. Melchior started to protest, his eyes searching the sky for the source of the flash, but both Jaspar and Balthazar were at their camels.

The Nubian chewed his lip, then grudgingly mounted his own animal.

Cold froze their robes to their skin as they drew away from the fountain of fire. The men shivered atop their animals, arms crossed tightly across their chests. Hours passed before any warmth returned.

Ever westward, the star preceded them, its bright white light somehow more luminescent compared to the yellow tongues of flame. Jaspar looked out past their celestial guide and focused on the billions and billions of pinpricks in the dark firmament—his mind only saw the tips of a billion other pillars of fire, glowing in the cold void of the universe, endless fires with no heat.

And one of those stars, he remarked with a smile and a catch in his throat, *had descended to earth.*

$

For several nights, the gravel stretched uninterrupted and they saw two more of the strange Wells of Fire in the desert, and each time they allowed the worshippers time for prayer. The gravel eventually gave way to hard-packed clay, splintered by a million fissures and cracks, pulled open by years of scorching sun. Two days later, the clay ended, and they proceeded through a dusty, sandy soil that led for a dozen miles before green returned, in the form of scrubby plants and jagged grasses.

Far in the horizon, the blue outline of a towering mountain range smothered the sky. Round tops, jagged peaks, and sheer outlines could be seen in the distance. A huge moon illuminated the small sticks of far-off trees poking into the sky and twigs jostled by a slight wind. Melchior thought they looked more like fingers— pointing at the hulking spires, jabbing, gesturing, beckoning, and warning them of a nearly impossible challenge.

The star glowed softly on the other side of the massive range.

"I think we have to cross," Jaspar breathed, his face lined with worry. He cracked his knuckles loudly.

Chapter 12
The Mountain – Trial of Gold

No temptation has overtaken you that is not common to man. God is faithful, and he will not let you be tempted beyond your ability, but with the temptation he will also provide the way of escape, that you may be able to endure it.

I Corinthians 10:13

The star hovered over the rugged mountains, challenging them to cross the dangerous terrain. Where previously it had preceded them, perambulating to the west, now it hung still; the soft glowing arms of the cross dipped, coating the peak of the mountain in its perfect light.

Jaspar's immediate thought upon seeing the stationary star was that of a wizened scholar patiently awaiting a response from his pupil, arms crossed. *But the mountain,* Jaspar reminded himself, *the mountain would give nothing*—*would easily cast them aside as ants.* Could there possibly be a way over this mountain? What sort of test was this?

Balthazar's retainers murmured nervously as the long caravan approached the rolling foothills, and with each step toward the mountain, it towered ever higher into the sky. Daylight would soon break on the eastern horizon, allowing for needed rest and a chance to inspect the barrier further. for now it looked to be a solid wall in their path.

Low, fern-covered hills stretched only a few thousand paces before ending at the base of what appeared to be slate-gray pillars of solid stone; these mammoth slabs of rock sprang into the night sky, ending in long jagged ridges. Higher up, the trees clung to a sharp slope upward before they faded away at the highest point, where tufts of a white substance pocked the granite surface.

The kings' eyes were like nervous hummingbirds as they desperately searched for any viable passageway through the mountain. From their vantage point, they saw no cuts in the rock, or any trail along a ridge—it seemed to be a dead end.

Yet the star still hung high above the mountain. Waiting.

"It's best if we get close and set camp," Balthazar said. "I don't want to try to climb this mountain at night."

If we can climb it at all, Melchior thought with a scowl. They had no equipment or skill at such a dangerous venture—what of the retainers, the animals? He looked back along the trail, then again at the mountain. *So be it.* "Indeed. Indeed," he said. "I believe we can rest for a day without the star moving; we've seen it wait for us before." He bit his lip. "But, is there any way we can go around this range and still pick up the star?"

Balthazar nodded.

The ruler of Tharsis nodded and opened his mouth to offer an idea, but Balthazar's servant had sprinted forward, panting. Melchior called Jaspar over to inspect a strange-looking bush while Balthazar and Nador spoke.

"Your Majesty, the others, they wish to wait until daylight to go up. Some are afraid of the heights, and it is dark."

"This, we were just discussing. We agree, Nador," Balthazar answered, putting an arm on Nador's shoulder. "It looks like we won't reach the base for another hour, but we will stop and rest. Daylight is coming, but we need strength. Have your men set up an area where we can be comfortable for a full day."

"Thank you," he said, starting to make his way back to the camp when his leader spoke again.

"Nador?"

"Yes?"

"Would you be able to scout along the edges of this mountain? Wake early if you can, but do not journey too far—it looks like it goes on forever." His head swiveled north, then south, and he frowned. "But can you at least do us the favor and see if you can find an end to this thing?"

Nador nodded. His eyes never left his king.

"Thank you. You can take some men if you would like."

Nador turned, started back toward the others, but planted a foot and turned to face Balthazar. "Maj—Bal—there is one thing, actually." He bowed gracefully.

"Yes, is there something else?"

"Y-yes, Majesty—er, yes. There is something…" He fell silent again. The B of Balthazar was barely formed on his lips. Nador darted a nervous glance at Jaspar, then Melchior, both of whom were still chatting about the strange plant, every so often pointing at the mountain.

"Yes, what is it?"

Nador fidgeted. "Er… I have heard you speaking with these men before, and it does not bother me, but—" He stopped suddenly, his face full of shame.

"Please, you may share anything with me. There is nothing to be ashamed about. We talk of many things that are not so easily understood." He did not want to sound arrogant and breathed a sigh of relief when the servant shook his head fervently.

"N-no, that is not it. I will never understand the things you speak of, about the stars, but to be truthful..."

"Yes?"

"I do not understand you *at all* when you speak to these men!" He blurted the last sentence, colored briefly, but quickly recovered himself, looking intensely relieved of a heavy burden.

"You do not understand us at all?"

"No. Not a word."

"Not a single word?" Balthazar looked confused. "But you understand what I am saying now?"

The man nodded.

"I see." Balthazar pinched his ear and scowled. *He doesn't understand...* "Not a word? Not one?"

"Not a single one; it is as if you are all speaking a language I do not understand."

Balthazar balled his fists and unclenched them. He took in a wave of clean mountain air and let it out slowly. "Not a—" He broke off and shook his head, whispering under his breath. Looking up, he squared his shoulders and sighed. "You had best be on your way."

Nador nodded and sprinted away.

Balthazar stood, scratching his head beneath his thick turban.

The ruler of Saba walked to his companions. They stood, looking strangely relaxed against the backdrop of the unforgiving mountain. "He says he can't understand us," he said, shaking his head. "That none of the staff can understand a word we say."

"They can't understand a single word we say?" Jaspar asked. He cracked his knuckles. "At all?"

Balthazar shook his head.

"That is curious. Curious," Melchior said softly.

Jaspar scratched his beard. "Well... It would explain the strange looks we've received over the years, especially when we first met." He fidgeted with his turban. "But how can we understand one another?"

His companions shrugged simultaneously.

The turban went back up with a jerk as he tugged furiously on his ear, and a deep and thoughtful frown pulled the sides of his mouth downward. "So what language *are* we even speaking, if we can understand one another?" Balthazar spluttered.

To that question, the great and highly intelligent astronomers had no answer.

§

Nador returned with bad news—the range stretched for miles in either direction, ending at a thick forest to the north, and a seemingly bottomless canyon to the south. Balthazar ordered him to pack up the camp so they could start toward the mountain; it would be difficult for his servant without sleep, but they were all making sacrifices.

Balthazar assumed Melchior had not slept at all during the night—he had sat in the grass, chewing on a blade, staring up at the looming mountain when Balthazar had retired and when he awoke, Melchior was still in the same position.

After sleeping until mid-morning, Jaspar and Melchior walked toward the seemingly trackless mountain face. They crossed the crest of a grass- and fern-covered hillock that seemed to end directly against the wall of stone. As they neared the mountain, however, they noticed the hill dipped quickly into a sort of oblong flood plain or dry lakebed. At the far end of the gravel-strewn depression, a narrow trail burrowed its way between two round boulders, each half the size of Balthazar's palace. From this point forward, the path was unseen, only recognizable from the cleft that wended along the mountain in a switchback pattern. A third of the way up the face, the kings could see the trail proper as it followed a ridge and then angled up and out of sight.

"What a safe-looking path," Melchior muttered.

Balthazar grinned briefly at the sarcasm. "At least it is a path." The kings guided the long caravan carefully along the small path. The going was painfully slow, even on the level terrain, for the animals and handlers alike were not used to such uneven and vertical ground. When they passed between the large boulders, the smell of must and damp rock filled the air, and the daylight was nearly swallowed. The giant slabs of granite fused only a dozen feet above their heads. The cool air felt strange and cloying on unshaven faces.

The terrain did not improve once they cleared the tunnel through the rock—stubby fir trees grew along the edge, their gnarly and crooked-finger roots stuck up in inopportune places, tripping hooves and feet. Balthazar's camel nearly knocked him off the mountain before he could caress its furry neck and soothe the large animal.

Forward progress was a measure of inches gained and yards lost.

Rocks tumbled underfoot in a cloud of dust and the sickening sound of boulders as they careened off the sheer cliff face. It was a sound that would become all too common on their journey up the mountain. Camels shifted nervously while their handlers did their best to pacify and comfort them. The path that wended dangerously up the slope of the mountain was no wider than a man's shoulders and the travelers struggled to pull carts and guide animals and keep themselves from hurling off the edge. Eyes darted nervously at the trail for signs of decay, every so often warning shouts would burst out into the chill air, and even a few curses could be heard as men lost footing and panicked.

Looking ahead on the trail, Jaspar felt a wave of despair wash over him. The razor-thin trail bent upward at an impossible angle and seemed to disappear. *But why would the trail end...?*

"The trail ends," Balthazar said sadly as he followed Jaspar's gaze.

Melchior nodded grimly. "I doubt that it ends," he said with finality. "We will not be abandoned!" the Nubian yelped. He walked ahead a few paces, then scrambled up the steep incline, and his footfalls sparked a shower of small pebbles and dust. The other two kings coughed and waved away the cloud, watching in wonder as their companion cleared the rise and disappeared.

As his friend bounded out of sight, Balthazar thought back on Melchior's overnight stay in the grass. In the morning, he had looked resigned, almost defeated by the mountain—and now he leapt with purposeful energy. *What has happened to him?*

Jaspar likewise saw the shift in temperament. Something had shifted inside the Nubian, his melancholy now transformed into determination. But was it really melancholy or had the determination been building inside of him the night he spent watching the star? The King of Tharsis remarked how quickly they were being transformed by their journey. *The journey or God?* he wondered.

Balthazar glanced at Jaspar and the two stepped nervously forward, but Melchior's disembodied voice floated up from the other side of the hillock. "It continues here. It dips down and then curves around that big rock there." From their vantage point they could see nothing. "I think it's a little flatter from there on; at least until we go—hey!"

Frantic footsteps sent more rubble falling down into an endless void before Melchior's voice floated up. "It starts to descend past this point! Yes!" he was very excited. "I can see the trail as it winds down through some trees. We are near the top!"

Balthazar smiled.

It took another hour to move the first half of the caravan over the steep rise and along the trail. The kings retained the lead, moving slowly forward along a somewhat flat trail. After rounding a bend, they found themselves on another level section of trail, though a small rise hid their view. After pushing forward a few hundred paces, the three kings kicked up another cloud of debris as they screeched to a halt.

A man stood in the middle of the trail.

$

He shone like gold, garbed in a flowing and shiny robe of fine silk, his skin tanned to a gilded sheen, and eyes like glowing coals blazed from rounded sockets. Smooth brown hands with long, elegant fingers protruded from the folds of the robe, and his feet were covered with shiny leather sandals. Atop his elongated head, a shock of jet-black hair streaked back into a mane, tied with a leather strap; his beard was perfectly trimmed and short, with nary a stray hair jutting from the carpet. Bright eyes twinkled behind deep sockets, turning from black to light blue to indigo, then finally, back to black.

A nervous thought struck Balthazar, and he turned around to see Nador crest the small rise, face ashen. The King of Saba tried to wave him off, but the head servant was frantically calling Balthazar toward him; with a sigh, he scrambled back to Nador.

"Do you see him?"

"Yes," Nador hissed, glancing at the stranger.

"Then, then what—?"

"Be very careful, Your Majesty," Nador said softly. "I will tell the others to rest and go no farther." His voice was stern and edged with fear. "Beware the Devil and his cunning." He turned and walked back over the rise.

Balthazar turned abruptly as the strange golden man addressed them in a liquid yet booming voice, nauseating but soothing. He could not help but direct his full attention to the stranger.

"I greet you warmly, my dear friends," the stranger purred. His voice flowed smooth and melodic; it gushed forth from his bright red lips like a gently gurgling brook. In its apparent gentleness, however, Balthazar could sense a masked power, a deep and raging current.

Balthazar stepped forward and his companions parted eagerly. For all of the stranger's charm and allure, each man felt a dark edge to him, something indecent and wrong. "And just what are you doing on this mountain?" the King of Saba asked, his hands balled into fists at his sides.

The golden smile faltered for a brief second, but returned to its brilliance. The stranger's eyes glowed sharply in the bright sun. Jaspar looked deep into those eyes and swore he saw motion, something moving, and to his horror found himself being sucked into a rotating, whirling vortex. With effort, he tore his gaze away from the hypnotic face, and the stranger sighed softly, still forcing the wide smile upon his lips. "Why, my friends, I have been waiting for you, waiting to guide you. For, I, too, have seen the star."

Jaspar started at that and he returned his gaze to the stranger, careful to avoid the eyes. Melchior likewise pulled his gaze away from the color-changing pits and instead focused on the man's golden forehead, but even the tiny creases in the bronze skin seemed to whirl and spin, pulling gently but firmly at their souls. As hard as they tried to separate from the tension, the harder it seemed to pull at them.

"Is it not obvious?" The man gestured broadly to the east, where the star would be shining at night. As he did so, his robe lifted up and away from his body. From his vantage point, Melchior could see into the opening of the folds and nearly stumbled. Beneath the golden, flowing garment, the man's skin was gray. Not as pale as a Northman, or diseased with a plague, but the chalk color of the dead!

"No, it isn't," Melchior replied coldly. He tried to force a stern face, but he nearly chewed completely through his lower lip. "It isn't," he repeated in a whisper.

"Oh, but it is quite clear," the stranger's voice poured out into the dusty air. They were at a high enough altitude where breezes were cold, but strangely, the foreign leaders felt a sudden radiant heat as the man sighed heavily.

He is the Devil, Balthazar thought, as the pit in his stomach seemed to balloon into a coconut.

"The star is indeed a portent of great things to come, my friends," the stranger stated with his silky voice. "Very great. But not as great as what I can give you."

"What could you possibly give us?" Balthazar asked sternly.

"Everything." The man gestured simply. When again the golden folds of his robe bared his flesh, the faded wasp-nest color was clearly visible. "I can offer you everything."

"We have more than we need," Melchior said quietly. Their caravan stretched far behind them, carts loaded with their provisions, and with it, the fair amount of gold the king had hauled along. "What possessions could you offer us?" Even as he asked, his skin tingled as he had a brief premonition of what the stranger would say.

"It is not possessions I offer you." He chuckled, his laugh like dead leaves scraping along a stone path. "I offer you everything. *Everything.*"

"I said, we—"

"*Everything,*" he insisted, his voice silk once again. As he spoke, Jaspar could not help but find himself mesmerized by the voice and its steady and smooth cadence. Avoiding the glowing eyes did little good, for the voice itself seemed to pull at Jaspar and tow him down into a swirling current from which escape was uncertain. No, impossible. "Look out, far out from this mountain. Do you not see? I offer all of it to you. Out there, in the great beyond, are cities and empires as yet unknown to you—still, they overflow with riches and treasures immeasurable. To you I give these. And you will be their supreme leaders, for I will bend the minds of men to your will and subjugate all living creatures to your demands.

"Do you think you have gold? You will have gold uncountable, more bullion than the coffers of the pharaohs can hold. Jewels to rival the number of the stars will be in your possession, finery enough to fill small lakes, and women—women as you have never seen. Beauties that make mountains blush and rivers divert course so they do not view the stunning beauty of their perfect faces."

At the mention of women, Balthazar seemed to snap out of his trance. Like his companions, he had no heir to his kingdom, something perhaps their would-be usurpers could also latch onto. In their view, they felt no need to be called away to pleasures of the flesh, for knowledge and dedication to understanding the heavens and ancient philosophies were far more important. They dedicated themselves to a higher desire for knowledge and truth and sought deeply for fulfillment beyond any earthly need. Melchior, Jaspar, and Balthazar each knew there was something more to life, and to existence, a higher purpose that many did not see. And surely this need was a catalyst in their following a star.

Women? Power? Money? More kingdoms to rule? No, they did not share such a need.

Balthazar nearly stumbled at the words, and a wide, cunning grin spread across the golden man's face. *He thinks he has won,* the ruler of Saba thought, regaining his composure and straightened. "Get behind us. Get behind us and do not bother us again."

The look from Melchior was one of concern. Perhaps it was dangerous to talk to this man in such a manner. Golden smile, shining eyes, and outstretched arms could easily mask a terrible violence. There were three men against one, but if he were indeed as Melchior and his companions feared, the consequences could be dire.

"Get...?" The golden man could not suppress the look of confusion on his shining face. Or had he merely given that impression? "I don't understand," he continued, palms up. "Take another look—I could even show you this if you followed. Gold, jewels, silver, cities and entire nations could be yours forever."

"At what cost?" Melchior asked. "What price does one pay for such extravagance? What price?"

"Why, it is a very small price," the man purred. "But, listen, you must stop following this star. It will lead you to your damnation!"

"And you won't?" Melchior muttered under his breath.

The golden man sneered slightly, but recovered himself, his full golden smile wide across his face. "You must give your hearts and souls over to me... for in order to bend the world to your will, I must be able to use your souls."

The Devil, indeed.

"Our souls and our hearts belong to none but ourselves, certainly," Jaspar said firmly.

The golden man turned his pristine gaze upon the ruler of Tharsis. He did not smile, but his eyes drilled into Jaspar's. Suddenly, the ruler's head felt heavy and viscous, as if it would roll from his shoulders and shatter upon the trail. Blood rushed from his heart, coursing through his veins, and filled his ears with the roar of the surf. He was losing his grip and the golden stranger was pulling him down.

Melchior opened his mouth to speak, but the golden man's gaze was quick, and the Nubian likewise fell silent, his eyes glazed.

"Get behind us. Behind us, behind us." Balthazar repeated the words slowly, careful, in perfect rhythm, and with the voice of a king. He avoided those eyes, those tugging, pulling, deceptively calm eyes. Coughing, sputtering, he repeated his phrase. "Get behind us."

The man kept his broad smile up for a brief moment, but let it drop. He was not going to be able to convince them of anything.

"How dare you deny me!" he bellowed. Silk had been swiftly replaced with brimstone and vitriol. Pebbles shook loose from the reverberation of the voice.

Shrieks of terror filtered from the king's retainers along with the muted, calming shouts from Nador.

"How dare you!" Thunder rumbled from within the mountain and long thin cracks spider-webbed along the sheer granite face, skittered along the trail and down the slope. Wide cracks opened and the ground heaved beneath the men.

Balthazar looked worriedly to his companions, but they still appeared to be in a trance. He balled his fists. Avoiding the gaze of the man became a struggle: swimming against a raging current, climbing a tree with no limbs, or digging through a pit in shifting sands.

Anger, pain, cunning, trickery, and mock empathy oozed from the man in the flowing robe. Balthazar thought he could hear the coarse whispers in his head, repeating, *Look at me, look at* me. But with effort he kept his gaze locked on a stone ten paces away.

"How dare you—"

"Get behind us! Get behind us! Get behind us!" Balthazar bellowed in return. He could feel the stickiness of blood as the nails on his clenched fingers dug into skin.

"This star will lead to your damnation!" the man screamed. How quickly the dripping accolades from his silken tongue had changed to venom.

"Get behind—"

"You cannot deny the power, the power I hold, the power I can grant you."

"I can, and I do."

"But all that you ever—"

"I deny you."

"You cannot—"

"Get behind us!" Balthazar bellowed in frustration. It took effort not to yelp like a exasperated child, but he held his voice steady as he repeated, "I deny you. *We* deny you! Behind us!" The last word echoed several times across the rocks of the valley below, before fading away.

Balthazar could feel those cold, dead eyes upon him, but refused to return the gaze. He had nearly won. He could sense the monster's frustration as the King of Saba denied him at every turn. The only sounds in the cold mountain air were the soft whirr of a breeze and the tinkle of a pebble as it rolled downhill.

Jaspar and Melchior still stood dazed, eyes open and unblinking, even in the bright sunlight. Jaspar took a tentative step toward the rock, as if being pushed forward or pulled to the glowing man. Balthazar reached out to put a hand on his shoulder when a sudden rush of air knocked him to the rocky trail.

He rolled over to look up at his attacker. Expecting the golden man—the Devil—his fists were raised in defense, but Melchior stood, straddling him, his eyes glassy and face blank. Behind him, the golden man sat with his arms crossed, a thin smile on his face.

"You—" Balthazar began.

"Do you deny me? Do you? Do you deny me?" Melchior's words were measured, emotionless, cold.

"Do you deny me?" Jaspar asked from his spot. Balthazar's throat clenched as the king of Tharsis turned his gaze to him—his head turning as if it were moved by a hand.

The yellowed man's lips widened into a smile.

"I—"

Balthazar tried to repeat his denial, but both Melchior and Jaspar were talking. "Do you deny me? Do you deny me?" They repeated the litany a dozen times, louder, louder, until their voices grew into a deafening chorus. More rubble floated down from somewhere behind them.

The King of Saba squirmed, tried to back away, but his back cracked against solid stone. A stone that had not been there only moments before. Over the roaring chorus, the Devil began a high, cackling laugh.

I'm going to—my head, my head, it hurts... The wall of sound was a vice, a press, squeezing his skull. Balthazar thought he heard a waterfall of rocks and stones, but it was only the vibrations of the sound—the cacophony of "Do you deny me?" consumed everything.

"I...," he whispered pitiably.

His companions continued their chanting, though they stepped aside, Melchior to his left, Jaspar to his right. Balthazar stared numbly over his feet as the golden man stepped slowly toward him—his lips now split apart, teeth glowing, eyes burning. Red. Red, flaming eyes.

The Devil! I deny you! he thought. For a brief moment, it seemed as if the golden man had stopped, as if Balthazar had uttered his phrase. But no, who could utter anything over the roar of Melchior and Jaspar?

I deny you.

"Who's there?" Balthazar shouted into the roar.

Say it.

The golden man took another step. His robe had started to flow open, revealing the chalk-white corpse beneath; it seemed to bubble and ripple, as if a million tiny—

Beetles! Balthazar realized with horror. Beetles, or worse.

Say it, came the voice. Whose voice? He knew the voice... but who was it?

Death took another step forward, head thrown back, hair now loose and stringy. Strands of hair like snakes flowed in the wind. *They are snakes!* A hand reached out for Balthazar. He tried to slink back, bury himself in the rock.

If the hand reaches you, you will die. Deny him. Deny him.

"I-I deny—"

The voices were louder. A hundred, a thousand voices—each from Melchior and Jaspar—shook him, pressed his skull, seemed even to push the rock harder against his back. Closer, closer... the golden man's clawed hand reached out—

"I—" *I can't do it.*

Do it! The voice in his head was louder, somehow, louder even than the blistering roar of voices around him.

"I... I can't."

Fingers—no, scythe-like claws reached out, only inches from his nose.

Deny him.

"I deny you!" he shouted. As usual, the words bounced against the wall of sound.

Keep at it.

He could smell the stench of a tomb. The claw was almost there. Balthazar slunk back farther. "I deny you! I deny you!" He cleared his throat, shouted, though he could hear nothing but the wave of shouting. "I deny you! I deny you! I deny you!"

The claw faltered.

Emboldened by the emotion, he repeated his shouts, though it felt he were underwater, screaming helplessly. "I deny you!"

The hand faltered.

"I deny you!"

The golden man stumbled.

Do I dare touch him?

"I deny you!" Balthazar screamed; this time he could hear his voice, barely a whisper. He balled his fists, then turned them palm out. *"I deny you!"* he screamed, pushing himself from the rock—right foot propelling him forward toward the golden man. Outstretched palms struck the robe and he felt as if he were pushing against a bag of dead Boswellia branches, but he still heaved.

The golden man's smile went flat, eyes black again as he stumbled on the uneven ground. His mouth opened, but Balthazar screamed his own litany, directly into the face of the Devil, and gave one final, powerful push.

"I deny you!" echoed across the valley below as the Devil tumbled over the edge and cartwheeled in mid-air. Balthazar waited for the crunch of bones on rock, but there was only silence. *He has left us for now.*

Overcome, the King of Saba bent over, hands on his knees. He pulled thin air into his lungs in heaving gasps, tears streamed down his cheeks. After a few minutes, he stretched himself upright and looked at his companions. They stood calmly, watching him.

What do they remember?

"W-what...? Is he?" Melchior wondered, shaking his head.

"I—what?" Jaspar asked. "Was there someone there?" Each regarded the other.

"Yes, a man was here. The Devil."

Confused looks passed across their faces, but slowly the memories returned, and pale, wind-blown faces now looked dead. Almost defeated. Melchior looked as if he were about to cry.

"He's gone. Gone back to hell where he belongs." He looked at his companions with a mix of fear and relief... Did they remember any of their prior actions?

"But, that voice..." The King of Tharsis stared at the rock as if he were gazing at a shining oasis in the desert.

"Jaspar, snap out of it!" Balthazar barked. He grabbed the other king by the shoulders and gently shook him. Jaspar's gaze was still out of focus and he looked longingly at the rock behind which the golden man had vanished. "Wake up!" he finally shouted, and shook his companion harder.

"I... I'm sorry...," he muttered and shook his head. "What?"

"Entranced, both of you. Under the spell, the spell of the Devil!" Balthazar shouted. "Wake up!"

Each stared at their sandals.

"The star," Jaspar began, looking westward. "The star did not lead us to the Devil, did it?"

"I'm not sure. Perhaps..."

"No, Melchior, no!" Balthazar barked. "Come, let us leave. God is good. God has won today."

"God?" Jaspar wondered.

As an answer, Balthazar walked off to fetch Nador.

Where had the Devil gone? Would he come again to torment them, or even drag them physically into the abyss? What other troubles awaited them on their arduous journey?

Balthazar sighed and called after Nador. He claimed not to have heard anything, and Balthazar did not push him.

It was time to get off the mountain.

Chapter 13
Myrrh's Miseries

Like a muddied spring or a polluted fountain is a righteous man who gives way before the wicked.

Proverbs 25:26

Ｔhe caravan started out early in the morning, the first dull-gray streaks of filtered sunlight wan against their backs through the thinning cloud cover. Jaspar looked up and peered through the deck, searching; he noted with a smile that the star still hung in the pre-dawn light, pointing ever westward along the trail they followed. Soon, however, the low mists that hung in the moor awoke and rose slowly into the sky, mingling with the moisture from above and below, thickening and covering the rays of the sun.

Melchior noticed the change, suppressed a grimace, and nodded to Jaspar. "It's still there."

Jaspar looked up, cracked his knuckles, and smiled.

"It is still there," the King of Tharsis replied.

Breakfast fires were doused with water from a nearby stream and Nador took care to leave the site as clean as when they arrived. Though they saw no sign at all of humanity, it seemed improper to leave the place littered with scraps of food and dotted with pits of black charcoal. When the servant looked back, he nodded to himself—he could identify no evidence of their presence.

Morning trickled by slowly, with little conversation among neither the kings nor the retinue. The moor stretched on in its seemingly endless heath, trickling water, clay, and rock. The thick clouds still hung oppressively overhead, and yet the trail appeared to make its jagged way west through the dreary landscape.

"I wonder if we should wait until night again, or at least until we can see a sign of the star," Jaspar said around mid-morning.

"We still travel to the west, I believe," Melchior said. He craned his neck, looking behind him. "The light seems to be stronger behind us, unless my eyes are wrong."

"If the star indeed points west for the duration," Jaspar pointed out.

"Let's follow through this place a little longer," Balthazar said softly. "I'd never thought I would miss the heat and the dryness of the desert!" He pulled at his garments. "It is very damp here!"

Jaspar opened his mouth to speak, but a tremor deep in the earth nearly shook him off of his camel. The animal spat and snickered; the King of Tharsis hugged its neck, shared nervous glances with his companions, and started to speak—

The earth heaved again.

The clay path trembled as if shaken from beneath, pebbles unseen rattled and rolled into unseen crevices and depressions. Melchior's camel screeched in terror as the ground heaved beneath the huge animal, and the Nubian was suddenly tossed from its back. both animal and beast cried out. He landed with a thud on the hard ground, exhaling loudly as air was punched from his lungs; with a groan, he rolled over onto a softer patch of grainy-looking sand.

His companions spun their animals around, dismounted, and scurried toward the Nubian. Melchior tried to stand, but his trembling legs gave way and he stumbled to the ground. Again, he pushed himself shakily to his feet, took a step, and let out another cry as his feet sank into soft sand.

Melchior looked around hastily, eyes searching for water or any reason behind his descent into the earth; he appeared only to be in a small garden-sized patch of a dense sand-like material. yet, it was thick and viscous, and his legs sank deeper and deeper into the substance. Ankles, then knees slid into the slowly bobbing, grainy, horrible stuff, and his hackles rose. Eyes were wide in terror, his voice box dulled with fear.

Jaspar approached the edge of the small pit, cautious but eyes blazing urgency. His knees slammed into the hard ground as he reached out a hand; panting, he admonished Melchior not to flail or fight. "You're not going to drown—you're not going to sink," he breathed. "Try to relax."

Eyes wide, Melchior looked down at the undulating sand as it crept slowly up his legs and to his waistline. Balthazar stared in horror as the man sank slowly into the muck. "It's pulling me down!" Melchior cried. "It's going to suck me under!"

Nador came running up, two strong men in his wake. When he saw the struggling Melchior, he made to step forward, but Balthazar put a hand on his arm and reproached him. "Jaspar has this under control; we best not try to make it worse... Go, go make some tea." He had said this very phrase to Nador a thousand times, but now it came off of his tongue awkwardly, and he felt a fool.

"But—" His servant did not appear to hear or register the strangeness of the request.

"Please, Nador, please."

The quiet, calm voice was louder than any shouted order. Nador bowed his head briefly and turned back to the retinue, his companions following, darting nervous glances back at the commotion.

"Jaspar, I'm sinking! It's going to take me down!"

"No, no, it isn't," Jaspar said calmly. He spoke quickly, almost to himself. "We have these small pits back where I grew up. We called it fast-mud or quick-slime... Smaller animals would drown in it, yes, but you are bigger. It can't pull you all the way down."

"But... but I'm sinking!"

The light brown sand rose higher above the king's waist, nearer to his navel, and he truly appeared to be facing a horrible end. But suddenly the rising of the sand stopped, and Melchior panted heavily, staring down, watching to see if the material rose any higher. The king's bodyweight was far less dense than the shifting mire and would not let him sink fully, yet had his panic overtaken him, he surely would have been sucked under.

"There, there." Jaspar breathed his relief. Melchior had stopped sinking. "Now, can you move your legs?"

Melchior's face turned crimson as he tried to move his appendages. "A little." He grunted with exertion. "It is like pushing against a tree!"

"Good. Now move them slowly, move them around if you can... Here, I can start to pull you out, but you have to move very slowly, certainly. Keep moving your legs." He knelt down on the edge of the pit and grasped Melchior's outstretched arm. "I won't pull hard—this will take a while."

And so Melchior wriggled his legs as best he could, while Jaspar tugged gently at his arms. It seemed to take hours, but inexorably, achingly slowly, the Nubian edged closer to the edge of the hole. Soon Jaspar could grasp a full forearm, and finally, Balthazar took Melchior's other arm. "One more wriggle, Melchior."

At last, he pulled free and collapsed upon the dank ground of the moor. The lower portion of his robe was soaked clear through and covered with speckles of russet and golden-brown granules of sand. Melchior's hair was soaked through with sweat and his chest moved in great heaving sighs, overexerted lungs crackling slightly in the cool and damp air.

"Thank God," Balthazar muttered.

Melchior grunted an agreement while Jaspar merely nodded. "We've lost a ram or two in mud like that, and once a small child, bless his soul. Even Father got caught in it once. I came running, thinking it was the end—he thrashed much like you did, but one of our servants was smarter and calmed him down. That servant never had to work a day in his life after that!" He laughed a mirthless laugh.

"A second trial, it seems," Balthazar said to himself with a grimace.

Melchior rolled to his stomach and pushed himself shakily to his knees. "Whatever we are following, it appears that someone or something does not want it found." He coughed loudly and rolled back to a sitting position.

Jaspar sighed and sat down next to Melchior. He clasped a hand on his companion's shoulder, but recoiled and wrinkled his nose. "You smell like myrrh! Like the trees in late summer when they weep their fragrance. But it smells… No, there is something else." He wrinkled his nose. "No, it's the smell of—" He paused and recoiled slightly. "It is the smell of a tomb!"

Melchior looked up quickly, his eyes wide. "A tomb?"

"Yes, and—" His hand flew to his wide-open mouth and he stumbled backward. Balthazar looked first at Jaspar with concern; then he shifted his focus to Melchior. The King of Saba stumbled as if struck—he and Jaspar had been so concerned with Melchior's safety that they had not noticed his appearance, his face, his hands.

"What—what is it?" the Nubian wondered, eyes clouded with worry. He chanced a quick look behind him, but there was only the moist rock of the moor. "What?" he repeated.

"Your—" Jaspar said to his hand.

"My what? What are you both staring at?" Worry was edging into anger, concern to irritation. "By God, what's wrong?"

A thumb knuckle popped loudly. "Your hair, Melchior, your hair and beard… You…" He trailed off.

Melchior's mouth was open to demand an answer when Balthazar's soft utterance rolled across the damp space between them. "Melchior, your hair has gone white."

"White?" he asked, baffled. "*White?*"

Jaspar stammered. "Like an old—white, like, like a wise man…"

"Like an old man, you were about to say! Like an old man… I'm… I'm not that—" He broke off, his gaze dropping again to his sandals. Eyebrows once obsidian now pinched together in a bush of stark white. Having no mirror, Melchior's mind pictured a hunched-over elderly man, scuffling painfully down his father's corridors. A man who would be dead soon, a decrepit, ruined shell of a human. He raised his hands to his face and they looked old, wrinkled and rattled by age. Even the tiny hairs on his hands and arms were silver. Melchior sighed.

I've died... the Devil... God, why would...?
Thoughts raced through his mind. He opened his mouth
to speak, but could bring no words forward. His throat
felt ragged. He gaped at Jaspar.

"It's not—"

"Oh, it is, Jaspar, it is," he replied dejectedly. "For I
have fallen into the tomb. Tell me, Jaspar, this smell that
is on me, it is something you associate with the dead?"

"I—"

A wave of the hand. "Say nothing... I can accept
looking old, as long as I can keep up with you both. Tell
me about this myrrh."

"Yes... we..." He cleared his throat and glanced up
at Balthazar, as if asking the man if he should continue.
The King of Saba merely shrugged.

"In—well, we would spread myrrh and other herbs
into the tombs of those recently deceased. It gave time
for adoration, mourning, and a celebration of life. In my
lifetime, I have visited countless such tombs, but... why
would this pit smell like a tomb?" His face was awash
with confusion and dread. *And how did your hair
suddenly turn to chalk?*

"It is another test," Balthazar repeated softly, his teeth
nearly clenched. "Another reminder that we are indeed
following something magnificent. This must be the
Devil's work yet again."

"There was something else, if suddenly aging thirty years was not enough," Melchior said slowly.

"Age, you did not, my friend," Balthazar said soothingly. "You only look it."

Then why do I feel a hundred years old? "I would hope so," Melchior added instead, forcing his chin up. "No, there was something *else*. There were—" He stopped and clamped his mouth shut.

"Do not be afraid," Balthazar reassured him.

"Afraid? No, I'm not afraid. I… It still makes me shudder."

"I cannot imagine the feeling of being sucked down like that," Jaspar said. "Or what it—"

"No, not that, my friend. Something… I felt something in there. As if hands were trying to pull me down!"

"The suction, I'm sure it—"

"No, Jaspar," Melchior insisted. "No." He bit his lower lip. "Not a feeling of sinking, but a feeling of *pulling*."

"I know, I—"

"I'm sorry, my friend, but no." He looked at Jaspar with wide eyes and he frowned deeply. "No, there were hands, hands that grabbed onto my legs! I could feel their fingers as they clawed at me, it—" He shivered violently. "They were pulling me down."

Jaspar opened his mouth to speak, but clapped it shut and scowled at the ground.

$

Though the moor was damp and syrupy, the sky was at least cool and overcast, providing a much-needed and extended break from the sun and heat. They had been able to continue through the dark heath, after calming the retainers and the animals. Melchior, still in a state of shock, steered his camel absently and stared at the ash-colored ground. For several hours, they traversed the craggy and bog-splattered heath, wending and winding their way along a path that more resembled a knotted piece of fabric than a trail across country. Through razor-thin breaks in the clouds, the sun's rays warmed their backs, but otherwise, low clouds floated above them and colored the land in a dull-gray hue. When its rays were seen lower on the horizon, the kings decided to pause for a rest, sending a scout ahead to inspect their path. The scout returned to report the moor ended only a few thousand paces away. They decided to make camp there instead of forging into new territory so close to dark.

"I believe we are fulfilling the story of Balaam in a way," Jaspar said as they ate.

Melchior sat quietly, staring into his hands, every so often brushing an invisible grain of sand from his robe. He had long since changed into dry garments, but could not shake the feeling of sinking in wet earth or of the hands. The hands, with their greedy, long fingers clumsily clutching with fervor, how they pulled, and dragged—

"Remind me again of that story," Balthazar said, interrupting Melchior's upsetting thoughts. "My mind, it spins. We've been through much in the last few days. Too much. Ba'a'laam? Ba'lam? Or Balaam, all one word?" He was careful to put emphasis on the breaks in the word.

"I have always heard it called it Ba'lam."

"I see."

"Well," Jaspar said, clearing his throat. "The translations I have are rough, and I'm not sure of all the words, but sadly, that is the way with many of the old texts. In any case, do you remember anything of the hill of Vaws, or Vows, or Vews...?"

Balthazar thought a moment and shook his head, while Melchior simply nodded absently. His chest still heaved in slow, deliberate breaths, though many hours had passed since the incident. The shock of the quicksand was still too fresh in his mind.

"Yes, far to the west, in fact, where we are heading. In fact," he repeated, seeming to answer his own questions, "perhaps we are... Yes we must be. In the texts, the hill was described as being the highest one in the area, and on this well were sentinels—watchers, if you will, of the regions surrounding it. Some called the areas Ind—but Inde as I know it, is actually much further east than even Saba—Chaldea, Israel, even Michean. In any case, if danger approached, they lit a great fire on the hill. But, more importantly, atop the hill, a gilded statue had been built; the stature of a star."

"I see," Balthazar breathed.

"And the star was built to spin slightly, so the gilding caught the sun's rays and also the moon's beams at night."

"Are you saying this star is the one we follow? That it—the one at the Hill of Vaws, that is—foreshadows it?" Melchior asked absently, staring vacantly ahead.

"It could be," Balthazar answered for Jaspar. "And we are heading westward... a little to the south, but toward these lands you speak of."

"Please excuse my harshness, Jaspar, but why is this now coming up?"

"I apologize, but it was something I thought of when I first saw the star—but we were too excited and I didn't get a chance to review the scrolls I sought. Though I knew they were there." He cracked his knuckles.

"Well, we've been busy." Melchior chuckled mirthlessly, again wiping his hands on his robe.

"We have, but still the story of the Hill doesn't fully answer the question." The King of Tharsis cleared his throat. "Simply because there is a spinning star on a hill doesn't mean that it has anything to do with our journey. It's a nice story, but it was only half told, to be honest."

"Half told?"

"Yes, Balthazar. The scrolls mention the region, full of diverse trees, plants, and animals. But then the text just ends." He acknowledged the confused glances of his companions with a slight bow of his head. "It's a fairly typical occurrence in the texts… *there were many other wonders to this Hill of Vaws, which are long to tell.*"

"In other words…" Balthazar chuckled. "The author didn't want to take the time to write them down, or they didn't happen. That description, it is seen a lot in the ancient writings—I would rather read the events than relying on someone simply stating they happened."

Jaspar nodded. "The problem, then, is that we don't know if the star on the Hill has anything to do with the star we follow, certainly." As if he had suddenly remembered another vanished thought, his gaze darted to the sky. Though thin gray clouds flitted over the moor, a very slight glow could be seen beyond the veil. Its luminosity was faint, but the wispy light that floated from the source took the shape of a cross behind the clouds and pulsated softly.

"The story, it still has relevance," Balthazar said after a moment of thought. "The star *has* come to herald something. We see it. Perhaps we are not far from this Hill of Vaws... but I think at least a hundred more miles?" He shrugged to himself. "Jaspar, thank you for the story and the reminder. We knew this, Melchior, that we followed a wondrous thing."

Melchior shifted uneasily. "I had not forgotten... I'm sorry. My mind cannot shake that feeling of being—" He bit his lip.

"Perhaps, if I told you in detail how we harvest myrrh? Would that ease your mind?"

His lips parted in a wide grin. Finally, the Nubian laughed. "It might put me to sleep!"

At that, the three shared a hearty laugh.

$

The moor broke into a grass-covered plain that stretched for several miles before giving way to desert again. Grumblings issued from the retinue as they looked out into the seeming wasteland—faces once hopeful for deep forest or rolling hills now sagged upon seeing the sand, gravel, and rock before them. Sunlight shimmered hot across the ground. Rivers of heat bent and curved in the far horizon, displaying a false image of water lapping against a dusty shoreline. But each traveler knew that water, shade, and food would be scarce going forward; the mirage was only a cruel reminder of the struggles before them.

It took little convincing to organize the large party into a gathering mission for food and water along the grassy field. The camels found low spots where water had pooled and drank solidly. Some food was found, and a stray deer was killed for meat. As day wore on, many men and women alike took time to sleep, knowing they would need to travel at night.

Balthazar looked out across the desert and sighed.

$

They rode silently into the cold desert night, guided by the bright star, every so often gazing directly at it, making sure they followed where it led them. Hours passed with inexorable slowness, and the rhythmic stamping of the camel's hooves slowly lulled the men into a half-awake daze. Lids fluttered closed, flipped open, then fell heavily again. Strangely, the camels seemed to keep an even course, even when a tired hand would pull the reins in a particular direction; the animals walked nearly due west.

A camel snorted. Melchior suddenly shook himself and shot bolt upright in the saddle. *What was that?* "Did you hear that?" he asked.

Balthazar seemed to emerge from his own trance. "Hear what?"

"I thought I heard something," Melchior said, scratching his head beneath the cowl. "Perhaps—no wait—listen!"

The others stared at him blankly, hearing nothing. Perhaps he was beyond exhaustion, worn out from the quicksand, or was hearing things in the desert, but he swore he heard a voice, a voice that seemed to be coming from the star. This voice belonged to neither man nor woman and bore very little emotion; it was rather the sound of an owl softly hooting in the dark of night.

"I am born," the voice warbled. "Born, a child. I am born..." And then it was gone.

"A voice! I heard a voice!"

The others looked at him, ears cocked.

Melchior looked down despondently at his saddle. "I heard it..."

"We believe you," Jaspar reassured him. "Perhaps it was only meant for you. What did it say?"

"That a child was born, or some such."

"A child!" Jaspar blurted. "So it *is* something new we follow—a newborn king perhaps? Or a new prophet?" He cracked the knuckles of this thumbs.

Melchior shrugged.

"There are assuredly prophecies about that," Balthazar said. "Most definitely. A child, hmmm? Well, that makes it a little more clear as to what we chase. The birth of a new king, a new nation, a child of God! All is possible."

"Such a star would not portend the birth of a king," Jaspar reminded him gently. He adjusted his turban slightly.

"Not an earthly one, no."

Melchior looked over at Balthazar, who held the reins of his camel in one hand and absently fingered an earlobe with his other. The king stared ahead, deep in thought. Perhaps he was right. They would have to consult the scrolls again, under the light of day; something in that line of thinking was becoming a very clear possibility.

A brief silence hung in the air.

"The star, it changes," Balthazar said suddenly. He gave Melchior a look of understanding and smiled. "I believe you speak the truth, though we heard nothing."

Indeed the star *was* changing. Its glowing upper region shortened, while the tail stretched farther toward the ground, giving it the clear appearance of a cross. Wide-eyed, the travelers watched as the glowing orb then stretched out from south to north, and within a mesh of peacefully glowing white light, the image of a child flashed briefly, before fading into the nether. And at once, the star collapsed back into its original shape, bounced once, and edged a hundred paces to the west.

"It was reading my heart," the king muttered.

"How so?" Jaspar wondered.

"After my experience with the quicksand, I began to doubt our journey." He sighed heavily. "I do not doubt the importance of what we do, but at times I worry that I may not escape this alive."

Balthazar's hand fell away from his ear. "Would you rather not follow?" His question was stern but respectful.

"You are not bound to us, you know," Jaspar added.

Melchior sighed. "I wish to follow."

"Then I am confused."

"Balthazar, everything suddenly seems much more complicated. I knew there would be danger, but the Devil *himself* seems to be blocking us at each turn. To get here, I had to bribe a group of villagers who wanted to eat me—and before that, I held my head between my knees during a sandstorm. All the while I had to worry whether my guides would steal my gold, having used some to fend off the cannibals. Those obstacles were simple compared to the cunning of the Devil."

"I would think that you would appreciate these obstacles the greater."

"I don't quite—"

Balthazar took a deep breath. "Sandstorms and cannibals are indeed dangerous. But would you not like to see what the Devil wishes to keep from us? If the he came here to stop us from seeing the star—or rather, where it led—what does it lead to? He offered us everything we could possibly desire and more, if only we would turn around and return home. Think, Melchior. Surely the Devil sucked you down into a pit of death for more than a pretty star."

Melchior scratched his head.

"We must be strong," Balthazar said, thumbing his earlobe. "We must be ready for the next challenge and embrace it. Balthazar is right. The star is good, and we are being beset on all sides."

"We have faced two challenges, not counting those we had to endure on the way here," Melchior said slowly. "There are three of us, and…"

Balthazar finished his thought, nodding. "And what is the third, you wonder?"

He bit his lower lip. "Each one seems directed at me."

"What?" Jaspar wondered.

Melchior nodded sadly and raised his hands, palms up. "I don't want to sound selfish, but I think the Devil is after me."

"Nonsense," Balthazar muttered. Memories of the golden man sent a fresh trickle of sweat down his back.

Cold sweat broke out on Melchior's own forehead. "It was vicious… the hands, pulling. Pulling. The Devil, in my head, screaming at me and I could do nothing." His focus faded and he shivered. "And the hands, the hands, the hands…"

Jaspar cracked his knuckles. "The Devil wants each of us. If we keep going, perhaps he will give up."

"The Devil never gives up," the now-gray Nubian spat. "We—I—I'm sorry."

"Why?"

"Jaspar, I… I don't know."

"I didn't tell you about the bugs that tried to kill me, did I?" Balthazar said hurriedly—the image of a longhorn beetle flashed before his eyes and the words fell out of his mouth without warning. He looked at Melchior with empathy and smiled slightly.

At that, the Nubian looked up in surprise. Balthazar nodded and relayed the tale to them, sparing little detail.

Melchior stared blankly ahead. "Can we defeat the Devil each time?"

"We can. We must," Balthazar answered.

The Nubian snorted. "You are convinced? You sound like a child."

"Then you wish to turn around?" Balthazar asked flatly, pulling the reins of his camel. Behind, the retinue kicked up a colossal cloud of dust as they awkwardly halted.

Melchior's camel stepped a few paces ahead and he pulled it back to face Balthazar. "I didn't say that."

"It sounds like you are, though." His tone was suddenly cold and threaded with a dangerous edge. "You have faced danger and survived. You have seen the Devil and survived. You have been pulled into a tomb... But now, even with the importance of our journey, you wish to leave. Then perhaps you should do so."

"Importance?"

"Of course it is important. What's wrong with you? I thought you were dedicated to following this star."

"I am!" Melchior insisted.

"Then act like it!" Balthazar barked.

"I just—" He bit his lip. "I *am* committed. I was just stating my concern over our safety."

Balthazar's cold tone froze. "You wish to abandon us?"

A low growl brewed within the Nubian's throat and his eyes were narrow slits of fury. Fingers clenched and unclenched.

"Please, both of you stop!"

For a moment, the two stared at each other and then looked at Jaspar.

"What?" Melchior snapped.

"Do you even know what you are saying? Melchior *was* concerned over our safety, and I am, too, but this is out of hand. It's another test, and it's right in front of you! Three tests, or thirty, who knows but God. And surely it's not God testing us now! You are both ready to kill the other man, and I won't have that!" He sucked in air and stared at his friends.

Balthazar balled his fists and opened his mouth, but slammed it shut as Melchior turned to him. He spoke, not louder than a whisper. "Jaspar's right, we shouldn't be having this discussion."

"No, we shouldn't," the King of Saba replied. Though his words were clipped, his eyes had softened, and he regarded the pommel of his saddle sheepishly.

"Is that an apology?" Jaspar wondered.

"An apology, it is. And, Melchior, I'm afraid we've let ourselves be run over again... Please, I hope you take no offense."

He bit his lip. "Well, I—" Suddenly he chuckled, his breath pluming in the cold air. "I think we are tired and it easily led to such fighting. Thank you, Jaspar, for keeping us from our throats."

Jaspar nodded.

There was a brief silence. "You will continue with us, then," Jaspar said. It was not a question.

Melchior stared into his hands and then straightened. Nodding firmly, he answered, "Was there ever any doubt?"

For a response, Balthazar simply kicked his camel gently and they continued along the dusty path.

Of course there was doubt, Melchior thought to himself. A nagging worry still nibbled at his heart and he wondered what he would have done without Jaspar there to stop him. Would he truly have gone after Balthazar's throat? His emotions were red and enraged and far beyond anything he had ever experienced—God would not stir his mind into a murderous rage. There was only one culprit. This drove him forward, drove him to the western edge of the world, through quicksand and dangerous emotions, and through the next challenge, whatever it would be.

I refuse to quit, he thought.

Chapter 14
Epiphany

Then Jesus told his disciples, "If anyone would come after me, let him deny himself and take up his cross and follow me. For whoever would save his life will lose it, but whoever loses his life for my sake will find it.

Matthew 16:24-25

Balthazar's sharp whistle shook Melchior and Jaspar from their slumber—they had been nearly sleeping in their saddles, heads bowed as the animals padded across the desert night. For several nights, the three kings had traveled across a trackless waste, while the bright, glowing star hung low overhead, bobbing gently westward, ever forward.

"What is it?" came a mumbled, yawning reply.

"A city, Melchior, a huge city!"

Their heads lolled slightly as they raised them to view what their companion was seeing. They had just crested a small rise and were following a worn path along the ridge. Set on a hill, the city had the appearance of sliding downhill, though the appearance was only a trick of mind. Upon further inspection, it had been set among a collection of hills, and the rise in elevation contrasted with the buildings such that they appeared to be losing their grip on the earth. From their vantage point, the kings could see the sun-bleached roofs of houses, and in the center, a large dome of a temple glowed in the starlit night, encircled by a thick golden ring at its top. Tiny sticks and ladders of scaffolding could be seen around the structure. Major construction of the enormous temple was underway.

Buildings of all sizes filled the spaces between the low walls of the giant city, from small stone huts to large, domed churches and homes of the wealthy. The city looked as if it burst at its edges, for structures, pathways, and trees pushed against the walls—even small structures could be seen outside of the city proper.

The star shone above the sprawling city, stationary and brilliant with a steady glow.

"What place is this?" Jaspar wondered.

"Hmmm," Balthazar muttered, biting his lip. "Hold on." He pulled his camel to a stop and dismounted. Dust rose into the night as he jogged back to the caravan, consulting with Nador. After a few moments, he returned with the servant, arms full of scrolls, teapots, teacups, and an oil lamp. "Would you mind setting up the table?" he asked Nador. "I'll go get a fire started for tea. The others can rest. I think we'll be here a while— perhaps into the daylight."

Nador nodded and scampered off.

They had brought very little firewood and instead lived on dried meats and vegetables, and so had little need to burn much of the wood, although Balthazar was careful only to start the smallest of fires possible—just enough to fit a kettle. The dry wood burned intensely, and he immediately dropped the teapot atop the logs.

"It's going to taste like smoke and very old water."

"At least it can keep us awake," Jaspar said.

Melchior laughed. "As long as it's wet, I don't mind."

It took more time to unroll and organize the scrolls than it did to get the fire going, and the rickety table was soon covered in papers. The oil lamp gave off enough light for squinted reading, though it also produced an acrid, rancid smoke that wafted across the table, fouling the taste of the tea. Yet each king drank the brown liquid, pleased at least to enjoy this one pleasure. With a city so close, restocking would no longer be a problem.

"What are we looking for?" Jaspar wondered, trading glances between Balthazar, the star, and the hulking outline of the city below.

"I think we'll know it when we see it," the King of Saba replied, and the men carefully unrolled scrolls, put fingers to beards, and peered at the texts.

Soon, however, enthusiasm blossomed, and scrolls were unrolled and re-rolled with care. As minutes ticked into an hour, fervor changed to irritation—scrolls and texts were now examined hurriedly, cast aside with a clipped "Huh" or "Not there," and discarded scrolls reexamined. Moods soured increasingly as this trend continued, without an item of importance discovered.

Several frustrating hours passed as they continued to roll and unroll scrolls. "I don't know what I'm looking for!" Balthazar said, exasperated.

Melchior's eyes went wide and he stepped away from the table. He sucked in a fresh cloud of cool air, and when he exhaled, his eyes were wet. "I know. I know!" he repeated, pointing at the scrolls. "I think I see something and then there is nothing. It looks only like black lines!"

Confused looks passed among the others.

"Is… is that all of the scrolls?" Jaspar asked, an edge of incredulity in his voice.

"This *is* all of them, isn't it?" Melchior added, looking at Balthazar.

"Yes, of course it—wait! No!" He clapped his hands together. "Nador put them all in one cart, but I had some more I packed in at the last minute, but they wouldn't shed any more light on anything, no more than these—" He stopped, staring at the table, his mouth still open.

Jaspar took a tentative step toward him. "Is everything—?"

"It's not in any of those. It... Wait!" Balthazar gushed suddenly.

Jaspar jumped, his heart missing a beat.

The King of Saba straightened and stared into the distance with huge, round eyes. Suddenly, he darted off, his feet kicking up a cloud of dust that caught in the ashes of the fire, sending up a brief wave of acrid, dirty smoke.

When he arrived at the cart, a serving man was leaning against it, dozing, and he quietly reached past the figure and pulled out a scroll of his own. He raced back to the table and quickly unfurled it, setting the teapot on one end and his full cup on the other. Small brown droplets splattered up and onto the ancient parchment. "This!"

"And what is that?" Melchior wondered, leaning over the table.

On Balthazar's left side, Jaspar leaned in, staring.

The scroll was timeworn and ragged, its bleached surface yellowed and tarnished. A small stain covered a few words, but otherwise, the ancient script was readable.

Foreign and almost impossible to decipher, but it was at least legible, if only to Balthazar. His eyes scanned over the document, and his mouth raced along as he muttered the words. His frame came erect and he smiled.

"What is it?" Melchior wondered.

"What we follow, it is written there."

Jaspar scratched his head. "What?"

"Friends, it is clearly written in the text!"

"I'm sorry, I know many languages and variations, but that..." The King of Tharsis pointed at the scroll. "That is nothing but lines on paper."

Balthazar balled his fists, then thumbed his earlobe. "Oh, I thought... Well, the text is very ancient, but it clearly talks about the star. Why did I not think of this earlier?" He scratched under his beard, then moved a hand to his ear—with the excitement his hands moved nervously of their own accord.

To himself he muttered, "I don't remember bringing this one, either... It was not in the cart when we started—oh well." To the others, he smiled. "And we were right about the Hill of Vaws."

Fidgeting, Melchior bit his lip. "Could you explain, please?" There was a slight edge to his voice, but he stoically held himself from barking at Balthazar, given their previous encounter, though containing his excitement was nearly as difficult as standing down the Devil.

"I'll answer with a question. Where are we?"

"Near a large town." Jaspar pointed. "Far, far to the west of Saba. I don't—"

"That town is Jerusalem, or Urušalimum... It has to be. Look!" He pointed up at the stars, indicated several constellations, and then assessed Polaris, where it hung low ahead of them. "I've sent men to this town before, though not very often, and each time they follow these same constellations. It's obvious, since it is the only large city in the region. So, besides the Romans, what religion dominates here?"

Both Melchior and Jaspar looked at him.

"I apologize. I don't mean to sound pedantic. So, the Jews are here, cast out from Egypt, not far from where you live, Melchior."

He started to speak again, but the Nubian caught on what he thought was a throwaway phrase. "And we kicked them out, yes," he replied, chewing on his bottom lip.

"We?" Jaspar inquired.

"It is a long and sordid story. The Nubians don't exactly have a lot of love for Egypt, but those folks do have access to the Great River, and as such, we are often forced to deal with them. Although the exodus occurred thousands of years ago, our family line constantly reminds itself of the fiasco—the King of Nubia at the time was forced into silence regarding the matter."

"How so?"

"Well, Balthazar, the pharaoh sent a messenger to our lands, stating that Nubia would remain loyal to the pharaohs and should we attempt to help the Hebrews, we would be cast out next."

"Cast out of your own lands?" Jaspar wondered.

Melchior shook his head sadly, his upper teeth a hair away from crunching down on his lower lip. "By 'cast out,' he surely meant slaughter, Jaspar. Slaughter. We would have been run over and killed. We had to shut out a small tribe—shut them out from our own land because of the threat… And so I, like many in my family, feel we were responsible for their plight and their wandering." He repeated "responsible" under his breath, scowling at the teapot.

Balthazar breathed out a cloud of steam. "There are some who claim the exodus never occurred… That the Hebrews simply resettled in this region."

Melchior chuckled. "Surely part of the pharaoh's political scheme. If they had 'resettled,' why had *everyone* gone? Why was it told from generation to generation, the painful lesson taught over and over?"

The King of Saba nodded and abandoned further inquiry. Whispers and rumors were flimsy pillars for opinions, something he had painfully discovered as a young ruler. But often, rumors could at least be trusted for a starting point, a reference from which to build or uncover more evidence. And if the same story was passed from century to century...? It had to start somewhere. Melchior's story had weight, given the sheer number of Hebrews in Jerusalem alone. He wanted to discuss the matter further, but they had more pressing business.

Instead, he said, "The burdens we must bear. Men have returned to me, their robes new and shiny, only to tell me the merchant I sought had died, and that they were robbed by bandits on the journey. Some of those men are still in prison. A digression, I apologize..." He paused. "This journey at least has given us a break from *those* problems."

"It hasn't given the Jews a break," Melchior said curtly.

"True, but at least they found a place..." Balthazar trailed off, thumbing his earlobe. He reached for a teacup, then pulled his arm back, his appetite gone.

"A place crawling with Roman soldiers, Balthazar..."

"Melchior, soon the whole world will be crawling with them, certainly," Jaspar said with a sigh. "They have it in them to rule the world and they are making a lot of headway. We have been lucky so far that we have not seen any."

"Our path has been across desert, mostly. Someday the Romans will reach farther east, but I can't imagine them knowing yet how to travel in the desert, unless someone has taught them to read the stars." Melchior paused. "Then again, they eat all night. I hear their feasts are legendary. Their displays of gluttony are beyond compare."

"We're tired and rambling," Balthazar said, raising a gentle hand. He rubbed his eyes and returned his gaze to the scroll. "The Jews have now found home in Jerusalem, and they carry with them many ancient prophecies. But one coincides with the Hill of Vaws and the star—while the King of Babylonia thought himself the next immortal king, it did not mean the belief in such a king had ended. No, people still believe that the next ruler would not rule by earthly hands."

"And he is heralded by a star?"

"Correct, Jaspar."

"Pardon me, but what is the excitement? I thought we understood we were following something like that. Or at least we had that figured out—no offense, but—"

"Don't worry, Melchior," Balthazar said calmly. "The excitement is because we have confirmation. We have a town—a great city, that is, in which we can ask other learned men for the rest of the prophecy. If we ride in without the knowledge, we look like fools, but now we know. We know!" He veritably bounced.

"Yes, Balthazar, yes." Melchior's teeth clamped down on chapped lips. "But you said 'rest of the prophecy'... Do you mean you don't know the full prophecy?" *How can you be so excited for only a piece of the tale?*

"The rest? Oh, yes." His eyes danced and his voice was full of excitement. "No, this scroll only says that the King of the Jews would be heralded by a star! See?" He pointed at the scroll. The others strained to make out any of the texts. They could understand none of it, but still looked on respectfully.

"'Though night still covers the earth and darkness the peoples, on you Yahweh is rising and over you his glory can be seen. The nations will come to your light and kings to your dawning brightness, bearing gifts and treasures of the far worlds.' Brightness! A star! What else... and kings?" He turned to his companions, face awash with rapture. "Kings! Three kings, we, traveling, following. Can you not see it?" He finished the last sentence with what was nearly a squeal and stared wide-eyed at the parchment. Trembling, he reached for a teacup, but his quivering hand came away empty.

Realization dawned on his companions with force. While Balthazar was talking, Jaspar had reached for a cup, and when the King of Saba finished, Jaspar let it fall to the hard ground; Melchior's bottom lip finally released itself from his teeth and hung open in the cold desert night.

Balthazar turned slowly to his friends and smiled with moist eyes at their expressions. "Do you now understand?" he whispered.

The others nodded dumbly. For several moments, the only sign of life among the kings was the slow trickle of steam that escaped their half-open lips.

"And I suppose I do not need to make mention of the fragrant herbs in this text?" He again checked their expressions, but they were still numb. "No... no. Obvious, it is clearly obvious. Clearly. Here is the confirmation of that which we sought."

Jaspar slowly brought himself back into focus and addressed the group. "I suppose there is no doubt, is there?" His voice was quiet and full of a hushed reverence. Slowly, his head lifted to the sky and the star's beauty pulled at him "We have found you."

Balthazar scanned the horizon, eyes moist. He balled his fists, thumbed his earlobe and coughed nervously. "I—yes, we—we—our journey is almost over. Come!"

Hastily, they packed up the scrolls, tossing them unceremoniously into a trunk. Nador found himself waking the servants and retainers, lacing his soft words with a string of apologies and promises for future help. The servants woke groggily, grumbling and a little bitter. It was expected behavior, and Nador masterfully calmed the multitude and set the caravan in motion once again.

As the caravan ground the teapot and cups into dust beneath its hooves and feet, Melchior's own eyes were slick with salty tears. He looked at the star and the city of Jerusalem ahead and breathed into the night. "We've found you. The King of the Jews... The King of Man!"

Chapter 15
The Meeting of the Ways

The king's heart is a stream of water in the hand of the Lord; he turns it wherever he will.

Proverbs 21:1

Less than one mile outside of the city, the caravan stopped. Jerusalem glowed in the distance, while the star hung above its hulking form, beckoning. For now, the companions' excitement over the newborn king was paused, as they had arrived suddenly upon a curious crossing of roads in the desert. The wide track they had been following suddenly ended where two others joined in, one from the southeast and one from the northeast, merging into a circular flattening of the terrain. To the west, leading to Jerusalem, a small trail meandered through the rocky countryside, fading away in the pale light.

Jaspar dismounted first and walked toward the expansion where the roads met, scratching his head under his tunic. He shivered briefly and steam plumed out as he sighed. "How curious," he muttered. Again, his frame was racked with a shudder and he huddled into his robes. "Cold, so very cold."

Balthazar sniffed the air. "I can smell the sea, but barely. We must be near Bar al-Rum, the Great Sea. There is a possibility that we will see snow... snow!" He gazed at the joining of highways with a curious eye, but made no move to dismount from his camel. "Can you imagine?"

"We cannot—wait!" Melchior's eyes went up to the other stars, something he and his companions had been completely ignoring on their travels so far. How could they have not noticed where they were going? "We have traveled by a very strange route to get here!"

"Most likely the star has guided us as close to a bird's flight as it could... amazing."

"Are you looking for something, Jaspar?" Melchior wondered suddenly, as the King of Tharsis still tottered around the desert.

"No, no," he replied, shaking his head. He paced slowly around the flattened area, and as he talked and moved, the clouds of steam billowed around his head. "This is very curious."

"You've already said that."

"But look!" He gestured at the ground, exasperated. "Why do three roads converge in this way? It is as if they simply end here. This trail over here is not large enough for a pair of rabbits! Surely it is of animal or human origin, and not meant to be used for travel. Why do the roads simply come here and stop? *Three* roads." He stopped and looked at his companions.

"What are you suggesting?" Balthazar asked.

"Well, nothing. Yet." He turned to gesture at the ground again. "But it is very curious. Three roads, three of us, and these roads simply end here, as if—"

"You think these were intended to be joined here?" Melchior asked.

"Why not?" Jaspar asked.

"I think you think too much," he replied, chewing his bottom lip.

The King of Tharsis muttered under his breath and continued walking in circles, staring at the ground. "Say, what is this?" He wondered suddenly and bent down, examining the ground.

Melchior yawned and dismounted from his camel, grumbling about wasting time. "All right, what is it?"

"Look!"

While the Nubian walked over to inspect the ground, Balthazar sighed and hopped off of his own animal, curious as to what could be found on what appeared to be well-traveled roads. A coin? Someone's sash? Perhaps a torn fragment of a scroll? He yawned contentedly as he approached, but his mouth nearly froze open when he looked over Jaspar's shoulder.

On the edge of the western-leading trail, there was a small pile of dust. A passing traveler would easily miss the pile, but Jaspar's seeking eye found it; a flicker of light from the star aided in his discovery, for the pile glittered.

"Gold," Balthazar said.

Jaspar jumped at the voice behind him, but recovered quickly and smiled. "Yes," he said, not turning back. "There is gold there, and look—a few dark pieces of... something."   ·

"Myrrh, perhaps?" Melchior asked, sarcasm thick in his voice.

"Or little bits of frankincense...?" Jaspar fell to his knees, pushing his nose close to the pile.

Melchior set a soft hand on his companion's shoulder. "No, Jaspar, please. This—" He bit his lip. "This cannot be what we think it is. We *want* to see it. Let's continue."

"Why would it not be what we think it is?"

"Because, Jaspar," Melchior replied. "Well, I don't know. Roads meet all the time. This could be anything, any type of sand or dust—it's probably not gold. Even if it is, what does it mean?"

Jaspar straightened and stood, cracking his knuckles. "Whatever you would like it to mean, certainly," he said. His voice was soft and calm, but slightly accusing. He had thought that Melchior's doubts had been erased by the quicksand.

Melchior opened his mouth to speak, when a sudden burst of wind roared across the dusty plain, bearing fine sand, lifting their robes... and blowing away the golden dust. He clamped his mouth shut in time to avoid a mouthful of sand, and each king bowed his head against the sudden onslaught. As soon as it rose up, however, the air calmed, leaving behind a hollow silence.

"Did you hear that?" Jaspar inquired, cocking his head to face Melchior. "Did you?" he turned to inquire of Balthazar.

Each man had paled as their heads rose slowly to face Jaspar.

"I heard my name," Melchior whispered. He shuddered briefly and returned to his camel. "I heard my name," he repeated. "My name carried on the wind, and the voice..."

"It was as if it were speaking only in my head," Jaspar agreed. "It filled my ears but also my mind... and with it came—"

"Warmth," Balthazar finished. "Warm air. I suddenly do not feel cold any longer." He paused, smiling off into the distance. "Come, let us continue." His camel trotted a few paces forward.

"Wait," Jaspar said. Melchior was already at his camel, ready to pull himself up, when he stopped. "Is this another test?" the King of Tharsis wondered.

Balthazar shook his head and opened his mouth to speak, but as quickly as Jaspar had spoken, he rebuked himself with a wave.

"No, no, never mind, never mind." He cracked his knuckles. *I think too much...*

"Perhaps the test is whether you will believe in what you follow," Balthazar said.

"It was comforting, certainly," Jaspar agreed. "I think I have been hopping at shadows, thinking everything is a test. A test of the Devil, certainly. I didn't think God—"

"God will not coerce or control," the King of Saba said softly, "but surely He has a way to steer our hearts, to present a decent path for you. And," he added, shrugging, "maybe a little reassurance along the way."

"We've had this conversation several times," Melchior muttered under his breath.

Jaspar rubbed his forehead, then cracked his knuckles. "It has been a very long journey. I'm glad for the encouragement. Very glad, certainly."

Balthazar nodded and looked down again at the crossing of the roads. "To me, it is very clear—we have been guided here, our hearts have been led, our minds freed, our eyes opened by this star." His breath plumed into the air. "If we had not heard any voices, we at least would have seen these roads meet, three roads that continue on a narrow path." He said this, staring at the small track ahead of them, wondering how the entire caravan would manage. *We have done well so far… not a man or woman has been lost.* "Very narrow." This last was muttered.

"Come," Melchior said, after a prolonged silence. He had turned his camel westward.

The star glimmered ahead of them, seeming to hover over the large city below, and as the kings approached, the star at last seemed stationary. The caravan had only gone a few paces along the narrow trail when a sudden cry went up from the throng of servants behind them.

Balthazar, Melchior, and Jaspar turned as one turned to see every man, woman, and young adult staring wide-eyed to the west and pointing with ragged fingers. Some fell to their knees, others bowed their heads, and most simply looked at the glowing orb with wonder and awe splashed across their dusty faces. As if in a wave, exhaustion faded from their faces and drooping eyes perked up, matching the glow of the holy orb.

"So now they see it, too." Jaspar breathed out a cloud of steam.

Melchior's knobby face broke into a wide grin. "At least we know we're not crazy after all!" *And maybe that was gold buried in the trail...*

"I wouldn't say that," Balthazar said seriously. The others each shot a worried glance at him, but he could not hold the façade and burst out laughing.

To an observer, the sight would have been incredible to behold. A mile-long caravan filled with dusty animals, people, carts, gear piled every which way—and each person staring and pointing at a bright star, burning like gold in the west. And their vanguard, at the head of the long train, three kings sat atop camels, laughing like young   boys.

Chapter 16
Incendiary Incense

I am the Lord; that is my name; my glory I give to no other, nor my praise to carved idols.
Isaiah 42:8

They were within a thousand paces of Jerusalem's gates, the star still glowing above them. Night had quickly been overtaken by day, as the dawn's first rays flickered wanly behind the caravan before splashing against the russet buildings of the city. Jerusalem now loomed—consuming their entire field of vision.

When the caravan cleared the gates of the sprawling town, the star seemed to dip and point in a southerly direction, but Jaspar discarded the effect as an illusion. Surely, this must be the city! Where else would the star lead? His companions appeared not to notice.

People filled the streets, pointing up and murmuring. Some of the whispers confirmed the kings' earlier hypothesis that the star had much to do with Judaic prophecy. Talking quietly amongst themselves, dressed in fancy but dusty and tattered robes, the strangers garnered a diverse array of glances and open-mouthed stares.

A priest noticed their garb and approached, his arms folded piously in front of his protruding belly. "Welcome, strangers. I see you are discussing something. May I be of assistance?" His demeanor may have attempted to portray an air of reverence and solemnity, but he squinted at the three kings with a look of mixed greed and contempt.

Balthazar raised his head and approached. Bowing respectfully, he answered. "Yes, yes. We see the star rising in the sky, a star that portends the coming of the King of the Jews." As he spoke, the star bobbed.

The priest raised his eyebrows and started to speak, but was cut short. A sudden rush of ice-cold wind burst through the open square and thunder rumbled far off, soon followed by a thick black cloud that seemed to billow out of nothing into a great, menacing blanket over the city. The boiling mass snuffed out the light of the star. No rain poured forth from the cloud, but angry and swirling vortices within its interior spun off smaller, slate-gray clouds into a furious, writhing mass. Even as a strong wind could be felt blowing through their dusty travel cloaks, a thick fog flowed through the square and then dissipated.

Jaspar gasped audibly, but Melchior placed a soft hand on his shoulder.

"I think we are going to face more trouble," he whispered into Jaspar's ear.

Jaspar nodded and regarded the priest.

A group of white-robed scholars sat on a curved stone bench only a few paces away, chatting amongst themselves in low whispers. The citizenry called these quiet men "doctors of the law," or "religious scholars," and they were the foremost authorities on a range of subjects, from prophecy to history, etiquette to proper farming techniques. They kept themselves apart from others, and were often feared or privately ridiculed for such action. Learned men, they still found difficulty in transferring that knowledge to the general public. And so they often sat in circles and chattered in whispers.

In their absorbed state of dialogue, they did not notice the dark cloud.

One of the scholars, who had seen the kings arrive, stood quietly and leaned an ear to the conversation between the kings and the priest. Words such as "prophecy," "star," and "wise men" floated to his large ears and he straightened suddenly. With a silent prayer, he excused himself, and went to look for a city guard.

"We are three kings—"

"—Wise men," Melchior and Balthazar said simultaneously. They exchanged a quick nervous glance. Balthazar continued, "And we seek the newborn king."

"Indeed?" the priest whispered and bent closer, speaking as softly as he could. "I would be careful with the words you use. There is a king here, indeed, already in command. His name is Herod... It would not bode well for travelers to suffer because they forget who the true king is."

Jaspar suppressed a chuckle at that. He was a king, true, but he never felt himself one, never felt he had supreme rule over anyone or anything. *That task belonged only to God, and whomever God sent—and according to their own Judaic prophecy, such a messenger—no, not a messenger,* he reproached himself. The star signified the birth of God *himself,* at least according to the texts. Thus, the true King of the Jews, indeed of the world, had been born (or was to be born shortly), and neither Herod, Melchior, Jaspar, Balthazar, nor any named king had any more right to rule anyone.

"We understand," Balthazar said quietly. "But we would like to know where it is prophesized... The texts we have seen refer to several different names..."

The priest dropped his voice lower. Hunched-over, eyes darting, and leaning between three obvious foreigners, he could not have drawn more attention to himself. "Beleem is the name you may have heard, but we call it Bethlehem."

The name was familiar to Balthazar, but only after he had heard it—if pressed, he was sure he would not have been able to reproduce it. "And this place, where is it?" Balthazar asked.

The priest leaned back out of his odd position and straightened. Forbidden discussion now out of the way, there was surely no harm in discussing the nearby villages. "It is to the south and east—slightly east, mind you."

"And how far?"

He smiled. "For you, not far, for you have traveled such a great distance. Twenty miles."

"Thank you," Melchior said. They turned to return to their retinue for the short journey.

They had gone no more than a hundred paces when two heavily armed guards appeared in front of them, arms crossed across their broad chests. The squat, muscular men were decked completely with sinister, shining armor, festooned with various trinkets and medallions. Round, slate-gray helmets, long sideburns of leather and metal covered all but eyes, nose and mouth;

metal plates, scaled like the back of an oversized insect, covered their arms to the elbow. Across their backs they wore thin black robes, clasped across their shoulder with another shining medallion.

As they moved collectively to go around the guards, one held a hand up while another gripped his sword tightly. "Salutations, my good men," the first said in a voice that was full of a snarling menace. He looked to be one who enjoyed his authority, and who would gladly accept any excuse to draw his weapon.

The kings pulled up and exchanged quick glances. By now, the priest had vanished.

"Nothing to say? I could not overhear that you were wise men..."

They stared blankly.

"Wise men or sorcerers?" the second guard said derisively. He glanced up at the boiling black clouds and sneered. "Seems that wasn't here until you three arrived."

How dare he, Melchior thought. He balled his fists beneath the folds of his robe and willed himself to be calm. Out of the corner of his eye, he could see his companions standing stern-faced, more than likely repressing their own anger and frustration. Why had they ridden straight to Jerusalem? If the star had indicated Bethlehem, and if the village was indeed close, perhaps they mistook the beacon as pointing to the large city, and if they had only paused and waited, and thought things through—but no, they had no way of knowing of Bethlehem, not without the help from the priest.

"Hmm," the second guard said. "A little quiet, aren't we?"

"We—" Balthazar started, then cleared his throat. "We surely did not create the clouds, sir."

"Ah! Sir, is it? Ha! No, around here, you call me Centurion, do you understand?" He scowled deeply, and an ancient scar across his cheek was stretched such that it resembled a great horned beast.

"Centurion," the king corrected softly.

His tone was not lost on the Roman guard and he moved to slap the foreigner, but his companion put a hand on his chest. "No, not like this. Herod wants to see them, and you'd surely be crucified should they arrive… damaged." He grinned mirthlessly. His demeanor was that of a mountain cat waiting for its time to leap upon its prey.

"Right. Like he says, Herod wants to see you. Follow us."

The three kings fell in behind the first guard, while the other marched behind them. The Centurion took a nervous glance at the sky. "Do you still claim that you did not make that cloud? It was not here before you arrived."

"We did not make that."

The Centurion growled.

$

Herod was a puffy, slimy man, his lips were greasy and bits of food clung to his stubble of a beard. He sat on an elaborate couch, plush red velvet covering a gold-plated frame, with various birds and wildlife carved in it. The man's robe had fallen open to his waist, and he reclined Roman fashion, leaning on a pillow. His enormous belly bubbled over onto the chair and bits of food hung on the roundness; more crumbs littered the sparkling mosaic below, marring an otherwise stunning scene of an ancient battle. Next to the divan sat a tray piled with food and various other items: Small bird carcasses, fruits, vegetables, various cheeses, other unidentified tidbits, and a massive goblet of wine, red stains running down its gilded cup.

Outside, there was a chill in the air, but unseen fires burned deep beneath the floor, pouring out warm heat through a warren of small tunnels. Thus, the emperor-appointed king of the region could recline shirtless while his subjects outside bundled in tattered robes. Each king repressed an urge to cover his mouth with the sleeves of their robes, for an intense aroma wafted through Herod's apartments.

Even for Balthazar, who was used to the heady aroma of incense, the bouquet was overpowering. *They must burn the stuff on the hot coals,* he thought, slightly nauseous. Looking at his companions, he saw a green tint start to edge onto their faces.

"Ah, the three strangers from strange lands!" Herod piped, still chewing on an olive. Wiping his hands on his greasy robe, he swallowed and beamed at the kings, his thick and hairy arms outstretched.

They returned flat stares.

He let his arms drop slowly to his sides, though his extended belly pushed them out and to the side. "I have heard you traveled some many leagues to be with us. That you have seen the star which proclaims the birth of the King of the Jews." He scowled slightly at that, but regained his hospitality.

"We have seen the star, and yes, we inquire as to its... to where it leads," Balthazar replied.

"Do you all seek the star?"

Jaspar and Melchior nodded. "Not the star, Your Majesty, but what it leads to. We are aware of the various prophecies and texts and know that the star does lead to the new—" He stopped abruptly, his eyes wide, staring at Herod.

The puffy lips curled into a smile. "King, yes. You can say it. Now this deeply concerns me," he said, pressing a flabby hand to his greasy lips. "I, too, would like to know more about this prophesized child so that I, too, may call my retainers and worship him."

Melchior shared a nervous glance with Jaspar, who dipped his head slightly. Balthazar saw the exchange and a look of concern washed over his face, but he replaced it quickly with placidity as Herod looked up.

The King of Jerusalem appeared not to have noticed the quick interchange and continued, his greasy lips moving quickly. "In fact, I have recently called in a number of priests and princes and a few of these men of faith—so-called 'doctors' of the law, and they have confirmed that the star is indeed a wonderful thing. I was a little worried, to be honest, when the star appeared and when my men told me that three distinguished gentlemen approached."

"Worried, Majesty?" Balthazar asked timidly.

"Yes, well—" He waved a hand slightly. "That is not quite the word, but we were concerned—again, I apologize. There was great energy that such a sight portended greatness."

He's lying outright, Melchior thought. *He's worried about something else, an invading force perhaps—*

But Herod continued. "It was said by these doctors, priests, and scribes, 'And you, Bethlehem, in the land of Judah, you are by no means the least among the leaders of Judah, for from you will come a leader who will shepherd my people Israel,' or some such." It was obvious he had put the exact phrase to memory, and as he recited, his lips curled into a slight sneer.

"It is such a beautiful turn of phrase, do you not think? I am much impressed with it, and surely as much as you three must be, for having traveled so far and wide to be here. Tell me, Your Majesties," he began, but the honorific came away from his tongue like a heavy syrup, "how far *did* you travel to see this new king?"

"Over a thousand miles, we estimate," Balthazar replied flatly.

"Far, quite far. How admirable!" There was a pause and Herod smiled, but his tone sounded anything but jovial. Round eyes lusted after the tray of food, but he stood still for now. "And so I ask that you aid me, since you have seen this star, that you inquire of this child for me. I must apologize for my soldiers who brought you here so roughly. It was not intended." Again, a wan smile crossed his slimy lips.

Balthazar cleared his throat. "Pardon my impertinence, Your Majesty, the Centurions, they—"

"Yes, yes," the overweight king replied with a wave. "They are all muscle and scowls, nothing to be afraid of. I am not sure they know how to use those swords they carry. I am sorry if they have frightened you. I can have them..." He trailed off and cocked an eyebrow.

Balthazar shook his head rapidly. "No, Your Majesty, that will not be necessary."

"Well, then." He paused, thinking, then went to the table and retrieved an olive. Herod chomped down loudly on the oversized fruit, chewed noisily, took a large swill of wine, and finally wiped his mouth with the back of a fleshy hand. No doubt a slave had been tasked with removing all of the pits. "I suppose I should call you 'majesties' as well, should I not?"

Each man shook his head. "No, we are merely astronomers from our own lands and we saw the star. Knowing it was significant, we decided to follow it." Melchior's attempt at covering his station was flat; the crimson tinge to his skin did not aid in his deception.

Herod's look of disbelief was sharp enough to trigger a catch in Jaspar's throat.

"Whoever you are," Herod purred, a brief sneer crossing his face, "it only confirms that indeed we are witnessing a special event. It was said you have come from across the sea?"

"In part we have," Balthazar agreed. "We are from three separate kingdoms, and have traveled far, over mountains, seas, great moors, and the hot desert. And along our journey the star has guided us."

"Indeed," Herod stated, disinterested. Another olive popped between his yellow teeth. "And you traveled alone, or with an entourage?"

"We have our retainers," Melchior said. "They await us outside the city walls."

"I see."

"Further," Jaspar put in, "we believe—"

"Yes, it is all so very nice." Herod fidgeted impatiently, cracked his enlarged knuckles, and drained his wine. "Now, please, I have much that needs tending. And if I am to give homage to this new king, I must prepare. Find him. When you do, return to me—directly to me." He jabbed a finger at his chest. "*Directly* to me. Is that clear?"

Balthazar nodded. He understood perfectly. "Then we shall find this child posthaste, Your Majesty. May we?"

An irritated waving of hands. "Yes, yes. Go. Centurions!" he barked. "Do not molest these men. They are free to come and go as they please here in the palace and in the city. In the meantime, start packing for a journey. I may need to travel soon." Herod seemed to have forgotten the three men standing there.

And so they quietly slipped away, through the bustling main area with the merchants and money changers. The kings hurried, holding themselves back from running, as they passed through two gates, a long courtyard, and into the streets of Jerusalem. Balthazar made to adjust his turban and chanced a look back—no one appeared to be following. He motioned them forward through the throngs in the streets, past beggars and unsavory bellowing merchants, and finally through the main gate of the palace and back into the city.

Part III
Behold Him Arise

And she gave birth to her firstborn son and wrapped him in swaddling clothes and laid him in a manger, because there was no place for them in the inn.

Luke 2:7

Chapter 17
Bethlehem

But you, O Bethlehem Ephrathah, who are too little to be among the clans of Judah, from you shall come forth for me one who is to be ruler in Israel, whose coming forth is from of old, from ancient days.

Micah 5:2

The three kings passed silently through Jerusalem, constraining themselves to a slow walk. Citizens milled in the streets; a few avoided staring outright at the three emissaries, though many eyebrows rose at Jaspar. He'd seen it all and worse in his travels. Today he kept his chin high and his eyes forward, not willing to expose himself or his companions to any further distress. As they neared the enormous gate, the throng of humanity slowed, replaced by the occasional camel-drawn cart or traveling merchant—past the gate, they still forced themselves to a slower pace, though the urge to run was strong. Who knew when Herod's thugs would come running?

When they at last stepped away from the city gates, the pent-up tension eased. "What a dreadful man!" Melchior exclaimed with a sigh of relief.

"He wants the child for some other purpose, no doubt. He's afraid of his power being usurped. Imagine, by a child!" Jaspar exclaimed. "There was such a system in our lands many ages ago, but it was put down. It seems unfair to—"

Balthazar held up an arm as two different Centurions passed into the shadow of the city gate. They stared at the three men. "Let us go," he said. "And speak no more of it until we arrive."

They trotted quickly toward the collection of servants, gave the call to pack up and travel, and were soon atop their camels. As their caravan eased southward, the haze and bustle of Jerusalem slowly faded behind them. Melchior cleared his throat of a sudden and began speaking, as if he were reading from a dictionary, "Herod, from the Greek, name which means 'song of the hero,' or 'hero, warrior,' combined with 'song, ode.'" He chuckled.

"That hardly describes him!"

"Jaspar, that is perhaps not his real name," Balthazar offered. "These Romans often give names to men to match what is expected of them—hardly fitting for the King of Jerusalem."

"Dreadful man," Jaspar muttered.

"Dreadful," Melchior repeated.

The next dozen or so miles passed in silence.

$

Balthazar coughed and pointed south.

"What is it?" Melchior asked.

"The star, it has returned!"

The light of day was fading over the western horizon, and with it came the rising of the star, pulsing with a soft light that gradually intensified, bathing the low-lying shrubs and wind-swept scraggly trees in its nearly white light. Scattered along this strange land were various caves, no doubt cool storage places during the summer and warm hovels in the cold winters—their black openings could not be penetrated by the brilliant light.

As night descended quickly, the star's light pulsated all the greater, pushing away the violet edge of dusk. Soon the orb stopped and hovered above a medium-sized village, not much more than a collection of a dozen or so buildings, stables, an inn, and a larger building. The light shimmered and bobbed, before hanging silently in the twilight.

"Bethlehem," Balthazar whispered.

They were only a few hundred paces from the entrance to the village when a few shepherds came running up to them, dusty robes billowing out, crooks held high in their hands, eyes wide with expectant wonder. Out of courtesy, the three men dismounted and brushed the dust from their clothes. Dusk faded rapidly into darkness, but the brightness of the star and the moon cast a warm glow over an otherwise chilly evening.

At once, the group of seven or so shepherds prostrated themselves before the travelers.

"W-what are you doing?" Balthazar asked. "This action, it is not necessary."

"Indeed," Melchior said.

Jaspar cracked the knuckle of his thumb. "Certainly," he whispered.

One of the men spoke up. He was perhaps seventeen and his voice cracked. "Y-y-your Majesties, we welcome you to our humble town. Please, please, come and see! This beautiful star, it—"

"Thank you, thank you, yes, Your Majesties, welcome to Bethlehem," interrupted a gruff voice suddenly. Its owner, a short and heavy man, had appeared at the side of the young shepherd and placed a thick hand on the boy's shoulder. The young man flinched imperceptibly and immediately forced a smile back on his face, beaming through gritted teeth at the three kings.

Wait! Melchior thought to himself. *Wait, we can understand these men, and they us… How? We did not understand Nador, nor Balthazar's servants. How is this possible…?*

Balthazar bowed slightly to the stranger. "And you are…?" He had had just about enough of men who felt themselves far more important than they had a right to be.

"I guess you could say I am the mayor," the man said, sniffing. "Though the town runs itself, there has been a great deal of commotion around here." He seemed to have forgotten the obvious, as he asked, "So what brings three esteemed visitors such as yourselves to our town?"

The three instinctively glanced up at the star. It was far brighter than it had ever been; by now the quickly fading daylight had been restored to something more akin to dawn, and it slowly pulsated its welcoming light above the town. Each king wished nothing more than to collapse upon the ground, being filled with an immense relief that the star had signaled the end of their long journey. But yet they still had a sense that their travels were far from over.

"Ah, I see, yes, of course!" the man tittered. "I forget the obvious, which I must say, in the presence of such esteemed royalty... Well, in any case..." He was obviously nervous in the presence of the three men and wrung his hands constantly. His authority was all but lost on the strangers. His demeanor matched that of the young shepherd.

"Yes, many people have come to see." The mayor opened his mouth to continue, but snapped it shut, as if waiting for the kings to speak. When they did not, he blurted, "I'm sure—I'm sure we can welcome you comfortably. Perhaps not with the accommodations that befit men of your, men of your, um, stature." Jaspar shifted when the mayor gave him a deadly sidelong glance. "I'm sure we can find rooms at the inn for you. And if not, I'm sure I could move a few people out into the stables."

"That will not be necessary," Balthazar said and sucked in air. "We have been sleeping in the field for many days now, and we are prepared to do so again. Perhaps if we stay longer, we may accept your offer. But it would not be right to put anyone out on our account. We are but simple travelers."

The mayor caught himself in a snort, but recovered quickly and smiled. "As you say. Please, think of our village as your home. I must return to deal with some matters, but you are welcome to stay as long as you like, be it here"—he gestured smugly to the rocky field—"or in town."

He left, walking hurriedly back to town, calling the shepherds to his side as he disappeared into the village. A few followed willingly, while others paused to look upon the three kings with wide, moist eyes before trudging back to the village in the wake of the mayor.

What do they see in us? Melchior wondered.

"I did not like the look he gave me," Jaspar said softly.

Melchior and Balthazar nodded. Quietly, they unpacked their belongings and set up the area for the night. Once they had most everything arranged, they walked into the small village of Bethlehem, all the while staring at the gently glowing star that hung stationary above them.

Though the star had stopped, they still found themselves wondering exactly which building or part of town it was hovering over. It almost seemed to indicate the entire town. Would the mayor have known? The shepherds? They may have known, but they seemed so intent on prostrating themselves that none of the rulers wanted to fight through the awkwardness.

"Perhaps that building over there?" Melchior pointed to a gilt-lined building, built from stone and some timbers.

"No, too gaudy," Balthazar said.

The star radiated such brightness that the entire village was illumined as if it were noon. Its cross shape was all the more distinct, hone points on the branches of the cross glittered like silver, and it pulsated outward, like a shining diamond in the night's canvas. Streams of pure white light floated off of the edges, tiny ribbons of unsullied wonder drifted in an unseen breeze, floating gently in the cold night air.

"It looks like it's outside of town!" Jaspar remarked, nearly exasperated. The star had paused on its westward journey only to taunt them again!

Melchior pointed ahead. "Probably just past that other gate over there." He bit his lower lip and added, "Should we move our caravan to that side?"

"No, it's probably faster to go across the town square," Balthazar said, gauging the distance with his eyes. The town wall bowed farther north and east along a ridge before curving back to the northern gate, and it would be quicker to cut through town to get to the other side.

They glanced at each other quickly, then ran. Ran like boys, hearts flamed with nervousness—they had traversed more than a thousand miles to this end, toward a finality they knew was coming. Though they did not yet see the final stop in their journey, it was so near that they wished for nothing more than to be able to reach out and grasp it. It was hard not to sprint.

When they exited the gate, they noticed the star perched atop a low building a few hundred paces outside of the city gate. This was still a portion of Bethlehem, but it had outgrown the walls; the area was limited to mainly farm and agricultural purposes with a few small buildings, stables, and animal pens lay scattered along the ground. The star hovered over one of these buildings—a nondescript, shambling stable, its roof covered in moss. A few sheep, ox, and ass wandered along the ground, every once in a while sniffing inside the stable.

"There it is."

"A stable, Melchior, a stable..." Balthazar whispered.

Jaspar's breath trickled into the cold night and caught the light of the star. "God *is* great," he whispered. Melchior smiled briefly at him, thinking back on the expanse of wilderness he had seen previously... From the magnificent to the tiny, God was indeed great. The three kings looked at each other, nodded, then returned their focus to the tiny, ramshackle stable.

"The King of Man, born in a stable, in a tiny, nameless village," Jaspar whispered.

The star bobbed once more, pulsated outward—and fell!

Chapter 18
A Stable

And the Word became flesh and dwelt among us, and we have seen his glory, glory as of the only Son from the Father, full of grace and truth.

John 1:14

The kings of Tarshish and the islands will pay him tribute. The kings of Sheba and Saba will offer gifts

Psalm 72:10

The entire star fell to Earth in a slow, measured descent. Rather than dropping like a meteor or comet, its energy flowed downward, as if being drawn in by the child within the stable. Brilliant white light from the orb flowed down through the roof of the stable. It gave no heat, but as it passed down into the crumbling structure, so too did its light, eventually extinguishing. There was a brief glow that seemed to come from within the stable, but it, too, darkened after a few seconds, leaving only the glow of the moonlight and the odd torchlight or fire.

"We have arrived," Melchior breathed. "The child is within, the newborn... the new—" He stopped suddenly, his throat again clogged.

Balthazar stood stock-still, mouth open. "My death, it has come," he whispered.

"Our deaths," Jaspar and Melchior repeated as one, voices hushed.

"New life, it has been born."

A few silent moments passed before they shook themselves from their reverie. "We are underdressed." Jaspar brushed at his robe, covered in dust and grime.

It took a force of will to tear their gazes away from the stable, which still seemed to glow in a bright, comforting light. Within, the shapes of the boy's mother and father moved, though now only cast in the reflected moonlight; shepherds and animals trudged to and fro in front of the stable. A young shepherd brought a torch and anchored it into the ground and the scene was highlighted in a guttering, sputtering yellow flame.

The three kings returned to the outskirts of town where they retrieved their finer clothing from a supply cart, which Nador had fortuitously opened. Balthazar's servant wiped something from his eye as he indicated the finer clothing. "Majesty, are you looking for these?"

"We are, and I thank you."

The servant hustled away to some other task and the three kings disrobed, careless of who may be watching.

Jaspar's attire was a stunning red, lined on the edges with a muted gold trim. His turban was as rich in color as the robe, with a burnt umber lining that could be glimpsed when he folded it properly atop his head. Melchior was in pure white, with no trim or frills, though the bleached-white garments shone in the starlight with an opulent luster. A gold-trimmed green robe covered Balthazar's form; the color of vibrant palm leaves, and the wire-thin gold trim sparkled with dots of silver.

The kings brushed away the odd wrinkles from their clothes, though Nador had stored them meticulously so as to reduce crimping or bunching. *He thought of everything,* Balthazar thought. *But we are overdressed and bring meager gifts,* he continued as he placed the turban on his head. He took in his companions and let out a small sigh of relief—they were not overdressed in the least.

As much as they had played the role of rugged travelers over the past weeks, they were still rulers of their lands and noble astronomers as well. They had for years worn finer regalia then they now donned, but a small part of him wished they had more to offer in terms of appearances and offerings. *Such a new king does not need any of this*, a tiny voice echoed in his mind and he smiled slightly at the affirmation, his hand moving to his ear, but coming away, unwilling to disturb his turban. Yet each man knew presenting themselves in royal attire would make the transformation complete—the metamorphosis from earthly rulers to a heavenly one, from kings of men to a King of Man.

Fresh tears welled in his eyes and he squeezed his lids shut. They were dying so that He might live.

Melchior brushed at an imaginary grain of sand, sighed, and started to speak. He was interrupted as Balthazar's head servant rushed up to them, out of breath.

"The others, they say—many—" Nador panted. "Many want to see this newborn king for themselves."

Balthazar adjusted his garments, delicately sliding the turban back so that the sparkles were not a distraction. "How do they know who this boy is?" he asked in wonder. "You have said you do not understand us when we speak."

"No, no, the shepherds. They have told us. This fulfills their prophecy—that now a new King of the Jews has been born!" His eyes were wide with excitement, twinkling in the moonlight. Even with the star gone, it still seemed bright. Balthazar shook his head in amazement. Nador had never left Saba, he only spoke one language—he did not realize he was conversing with people that he would otherwise not understand!

"Yet you understand their speech, no?"

"Yes, Your Maj—yes, I do! And we now understand their prophecy as well!" The man was overflowing with such energy the kings could not help but burst into large smiles, lips stretched wide. Nador's exuberance was enough to inspire a hundred-mile walk across broken clay shards or a long swim through mud.

"*Their* prophecy?"

"Well..." the man stammered. "I mean, Your Maj- well, I know... er... well..." Though he stammered, his excitement never faltered.

Balthazar raised a placating hand. "Yes, I understand. What you are saying, I hear, but what you mean is different."

"I..."

"It is not their prophecy. It is everyone's."

He nodded.

"Yes, we will let our people pay homage. But first, we must make our tribute. And when we are done, they should come, but in twos or threes. Not all at once."

"No, I assure you, not all will, but I will tell them to come in twos or threes."

"Do so, and have them walk with the shepherds; they will guide them."

The man smiled and trotted away.

"We must make an offering to this child, as small as it may be, certainly. Something from our stores, some riches." Balthazar paused. "Items befit a king. Gold, incense, myrrh. Items that are of us, dear to us... We give them as we give our lives to Him."

"Are they enough?" Melchior wondered.

The King of Saba chuckled. "We could bring Him a bottle of sand and it would still have meaning, would still be something of ourselves... This is God. Our gifts are both small and grand, they are birth and—" There he paused, moved to tug his earlobe, then let his arm drop.

A cattle lowed softly in the distance. Melchior looked up from his sandals, eyes moist.

"Our presence is surely as important as what we bring." Balthazar finished his thought with a catch to his strong voice.

Jaspar nodded, thinking back on their long journey. They had been through many trials, and trials within trials, in order that they could witness the birth of God. *The birth of* God, he thought, his own eyes filling with moisture. Surely, their offerings, as large or as small as they could make it, would be pleasing and just. Only the Devil, the Master of Lies, would measure them and find them wanting. The Master of Truth lay in a rickety cradle among farm animals, shunned from the pompous. Any gift to such a mighty presence... any gift would be plentiful.

The King of Tharsis took a deep breath, smoothed his red robe, and set his jaw.

They proceeded to the rickety cart, which held their "treasures," moving carefully so as not to dirty their fine garments, and retrieved a small bundle each of myrrh and incense, which Balthazar insisted on calling Frankincense...

"It must be given proper title, you understand," he said.

Melchior ducked into his laden cart and produced a round nugget of gleaming gold, shaped like an apple. He shined it on the hem of his robe.

"Where—where did you get *that?*" Jaspar wondered, eyeing the gold bulb with wonder.

"This...?" the Nubian asked, glancing casually at the golden apple. "It is said that this came to our family via the great King Alexander, though how, I never was told. My father told me that, though it looks whole, it is made up of small particles from tributes of all nations. Surely just a story, for I can't see how they got it all together. It is amazing, is it not?" he said, holding the sphere briefly aloft.

"Come," Balthazar said quietly, walking toward Bethlehem's entrance.

With that, they trudged through town and toward the stable. The three men walked one behind the other, the shorter Melchior taking the lead, his now white hair sticking out from under his strange turban in odd filaments of shining silver fiber. He carried his apple of gold reverently before him. Jaspar walked behind him, the red robe reflecting flashes of moon and torchlight, with the box of myrrh clutched in front of him. Balthazar took up the rear, surprisingly, after acting the leader for the duration of their journey. He held a coconut wood container of incense, his own garment whooshing softly as he walked.

Cattle lowed softly around them and the smell of animals was strong but tolerable. A few shepherds still stood in the immediate vicinity, milling quietly near the stable; otherwise, gently bleating sheep provided the only sound as the men approached. As the three kings neared the stable, however, each shepherd knelt low, leaning on their long crooks, faces cast downward. Balthazar wanted to reproach them as he had Nador, but held his tongue—it was not the time to worry about such formalities. Their destination was feet away, their future, the future of Man.

Although the glow of the holy star had been absorbed by the young boy king, the stable seemed to be bathed in a tender white light, far brighter than any moon, torch, or fire could offer. The chill of the winter night for now was cut with a soothing warmth. When they entered the stable, however, they were taken aback by the meagerness and poverty in which the newborn king lay. The tiny infant was wrapped in ragged strips of clothing, torn from garments long past their functional use.

The boy's mother and father stood by, and each king bowed respectfully, albeit a bit nervously, before the couple. No doubt many had come in the past day to pay homage, but the three kings were surely the most distinguishable and most unique—though the boy's parents merely stood, watching, as if the men from such far lands were expected.

The new king's mother and father wore worn but sturdy robes, their feet barely covered by ratty sandals. Jaspar glanced briefly at the mother and the air was nearly sucked from his lungs. A beauty as he had never seen, a pure, radiant face that glowed with the newness of motherhood. He found himself captivated by the love and tenderness the woman exuded—not a love as a man for a wife, but as a man for a mother, a sister, aunt, or grandmother all wrapped into a single entity. A perfect woman, a pure and unsullied grace, and a holy, glowing persona that exuded love.

Love. Pure love, Jaspar thought. It was hard to take his gaze away, but he did respectfully shift his glance, though the grace and peace that flowed from the mother nearly knocked him over—a perfect woman. *No,* he reminded himself, *a perfect human, a perfect mother, a perfect parent.* He ached inwardly, longing for the long-lost affections and care of his own mother, but the aching was swiftly replaced by an endless, swelling hope for all children—for the mother of God was alive in the world!

Balthazar looked at his friends and nodded. *It is time.* The same nervous energy filled him. His heart raced as it had on their gathering so long ago. Knees tingled. As one, the kings proffered their gifts toward the cradle, kneeling upon the hay-covered floor of the stable.

Balthazar stepped forward first, for Melchior seemed frozen in awe. Holding his head high, the King of Saba spoke softly. "We bring for the newborn king the gifts of gold, frankincense, and myrrh. May those who call your name be shown peace, those who follow you know God, and may you sow peace and unity in the world." After the words had drifted from his lips, he swallowed a lump in his throat—he had not decided that he would speak, but the words flowed of their own accord. He sensed the sidelong glances from his companions, could feel the warmth of their hearts.

And warmth and love flowed from the mother, from the father, from the cradle itself. *This is God, this is God,* he repeated in his mind.

It was a moment he had at once expected and also never dreamed of. Giving a major speech in front of thousands of citizens in the blazing sun was no match for the intensely silky, warm blanket of contentment that washed over him. He could feel each blade of hay as it pressed against his knees; the soft snap of dry strands echoed in his ears; the lowing of the cattle was a constant hum; and he swore he could hear the gentle inhaling and exhaling from the tiny infant's lungs. When at last he stood, he felt his soul emptying of all burdens and all past sins, flowing along its stream of purification were the dark emotions and the cold feelings he had felt toward his fellow man. Tears flowed down his bronze cheeks and he let them flow.

Melchior righted himself, his own face slicked with tears. Likewise, the dark and stoic face of Jaspar was aglow with rapture and release. A few moments passed while the men stared at the tiny baby, minds racing across the thousands of miles in their past, and the thousands of years that the future had to offer.

Suddenly, with a slight whoosh, the golden apple dissolved into a pile of dust, caught a tuft of wind, and blew out between the rotting slats in the stable.

Such a gift the Son of Man does not need, Melchior thought with a smile. *The apple is the world, and he has forever changed it.* His companions raised not a single eyebrow at the event. Instead, they looked lovingly on the infant. Balthazar opened his mouth to say another kind word—

A sudden gust of wind tore through the rickety stable, a cold biting chill, crisscrossed with snowflakes. Snow, and the stench of the grave.

The mother of the child was knocked forward and the father caught her; the three kings were pushed backward, feet flailing against a raging tempest. Balthazar dragged his feet forward, though it was like walking against a wall of stone—he was trying to get forward to protect the cradle. Though the baby's face belied no emotion, the meager bed rocked, buffeted by the onslaught of snow and wind. Myrrh and frankincense containers slammed against the rotting wall of the stable.

Melchior held his ground, but his mouth hung open. Words stung his ears, words carried on the gusts: *Deny him, deny him, Son of Misery. He will take away your power, your power, power gone, power taken, no more.*

Come to me. I own you. I have your power. "No, no," he shouted. "He is God, he is God!"

You cannot deny me a third time, the voice replied.

"I deny you."

The voice abated, then attacked Jaspar, who likewise shouted his defiance.

This will not end. I will not be denied!

Balthazar had only made it a few inches forward against the wall of air, his bronzed fists clenched in determined fury. He tried to scream his denials, but the wind coursed down his throat, and with it daggers of sleet and ice, which tore his mouth and set him coughing. The father of the baby kept an arm around the mother and tried to step sideways toward the cradle, but seemed rooted in place.

The cradle slid across the floor and knocked against the side of the stable, cracking a failing timber. Still, the baby's face remained peaceful, unaffected by the blizzard within the stable.

Balthazar raised his right foot to step forward, but as his leg was in the air, a violent current of wind ripped along the base of the stable, *pushed* upward, knocking him onto his back. He thought he could hear the crunch of joints over the storm.

"No…" he pleaded, rolling slowly onto his stomach. Tears streamed down his cheeks.

His companions had also been knocked back and down. Both the mother and the father of the baby stood, however, each wrapped around the other, buffered against the wind.

Melchior, Jaspar, and Balthazar watched with tear-filled eyes as the cradle was lifted slowly from its mooring. Terrified parents reached out their arms, but the howling storm knocked those arms back to their sides and they cried freely. Up, up, the cradle was raised, then slowly the snow-lashed fury tipped it like a tea kettle.

"No!" Balthazar screamed, pushing himself upward. But as soon as he was on his elbows, the gale flung him back against the other side of the stable.

Melchior and Jaspar flailed wildly, each trying to find traction to stand. But the snow had been blown in and turned the floor to ice.

The cradle tipped another inch.

Balthazar roared with fury and scrabbled along the icy floor, clawing and scratching for every inch; but there was no pushing against the punishing storm.

Sleet-filled terror tipped the cradle another inch forward; the baby was nearly on his side, at the tipping point. Balthazar screamed. The parents' mouths were open as the child began to tip out of the cradle—another nudge of the wind and the infant would crash to the icy floor.

A throaty, growling voice bellowed over the roar, a voice all could hear:

THIS ENDS NOW. THE SON OF MAN SHALL NOT BE!

"I deny—" Balthazar began, tears frozen on his cheeks.

But Balthazar's cry was lost.

The infant opened its mouth, as if yawning. The left corner of his mouth inched up on his smooth face, eyes opened to small pools, then larger round circles, reflecting sparkling lights within. As Balthazar watched, he realized the eyes weren't reflecting but *transmitting* the light! The infant's mouth opened wider, looking like an ordinary yawn.

He tipped another inch forward.

YOU WILL NOT DENY ME, I AM—

Balthazar slammed his fist on the icy wood as the cradle began its final, deadly tilt. But the baby's mouth was fully open and remained so—from the lungs of a babe came a shrill, piercing cry, not of hunger, pain, or even fear, but of proclamation! The cry was a baby's first yell of independence, a scream to the world that he had arrived, but here it towered over the roar of the wind, and it drowned the screeching, growling cries of the

Devil. Those in attendance were knocked back by the shockwave that shot forth from the mouth of the infant—Melchior and Jaspar were hauled to their feet by embracing arms of air, while Balthazar pushed himself upright to stare into the cradle...

...which had now fallen to the ground.

Snow still swirled in the stable, but the roar and the growl of the Devil were lessened. The infant's mouth was still open in a peaceful-looking yawn, but the air around him rippled. Balthazar heard another faint cry from the snow-laden wind, but quickly, the air was pulled out of the stable; snowflakes were pulled back and out of the gaps in the wood frame, and even the ice on the floor evaporated. The baby's parents rushed to the cradle, whispering words of comfort and adjusting his blankets.

Dazed, the kings stepped forward and helped to rearrange the stable, making sure to set the incense and myrrh containers in front of the cradle.

The baby's mouth had closed and he looked to be sleeping peacefully, though Balthazar still saw the sparkling lights dancing beneath closed lids.

"The world must not know of this attack," Melchior whispered to Jaspar, though his whisper came off as a hoarse screech. The father raised an eyebrow, looked at his son sleeping peacefully, and nodded imperceptibly.

The mother of the boy pushed back her blue linen head covering slightly. A single tear glistened in her right eye. Balthazar looked at her and felt a new rush of pride—though her face remained calm, he could see her chest heaving, and there was a tremble of limbs that jolted her robe. She was surely terrified and relived, though her outward countenance remained strong. The father put an arm around her shoulder and squeezed gently; she smiled at him warmly and he moved his arm away. After several quiet moments, the mother turned her attention back to the kings.

She held her robe with her left hand, while she gestured to the infant with her right. A slender finger indicated the boy's tiny head, and she nodded at the three kings.

One by one, the three kings stepped lightly forward and kissed the infant's forehead, knees still trembling from the event.

When they stepped back, she spoke for the first time. Her voice was soft and smooth, belying her meager surroundings. *It was the voice of all mothers,* Balthazar thought.

A voice that could sooth a venomous snake or calm a boiling ocean, a powerfully intense voice, with a clear, resonating timbre that consumed the entire stable, whispered, "Thanks be to God."

Chapter 19
No Rest

And he said to them, "Come away by yourselves to a desolate place and rest a while." For many were coming and going, and they had no leisure even to eat.

Mark 6:31

Exhausted from the day's events, the kings returned to their retinue outside the village. Not a man would remember the short walk from the stable back to the train of equipment, nor any of the idle talk they may have shared, or if even they did speak. For traversing that short distance felt as if they walked on air, pushed forward by gentle unseen hands. Hearts were light and airy, souls pure and clean, minds emptied of negativity, and eyes closed with exhaustion but opened by faith.

They wearily disrobed and put on their travel clothing. Tired and nearly at the point of starvation, they settled down to eat, dining heavily on fresh goods from Jerusalem. Nador had been able to procure a large number of items, though nothing as extravagant as Herod gorged himself on. Still, sustenance was welcome, and weary muscles absorbed the nourishment gladly.

"It is good to eat again," Jaspar said absently.

"It is," Balthazar muttered, tossing a chicken bone into the fire.

Shortly after they packed away their belongings for the evening, a shepherd from Bethlehem approached them cautiously. The men stood with creaking joints and the odd sigh.

"Your Majesties, it is said that you brought great gifts for the boy king. There are no other places to stay the night here, but it is not right that you should sleep out in the field. There is a cave—it is damp and dark, but it has shelter, in case it rains... or snows." He shivered noticeably.

Balthazar looked up at the descending evening, and a million stars had popped out across the deep azure sky, filling the firmament with an array of bright, fathomless lights—a cascade of starlight that was nearly a glowing entity in itself, a painted brush of stars. Not a cloud was in sight.

He opened his mouth to say as much, but caught himself. "I thank you—we thank you, that is. We will gladly accept the invitation." After sleeping in tents or in the open country throughout their long journey, the protection of a hovel appealed to them, even if it were a cave.

"Come, it is quicker to go back through town."

Balthazar, Melchior, and Jaspar followed the boy as he hurried back across the square. By now, most citizens had retired for the evening and the center of town was nearly deserted. They exited on the western side, across from the stable, though quick glances darted to the location of the boy. From their vantage point, however, there was nothing to see.

The cave was deep and wide enough that they could fit their camels inside. When Balthazar saw this, he mentioned as much. "It would be best, I think, if we retrieve our camels, and let them sleep in here—far back inside I think would be fine."

They lit torches, bid the shepherd good night, then trudged back to retrieve their camels. Once back in the cave, Balthazar discovered a second exit, perhaps a thousand paces outside of town on the southern edge. "That might be convenient," Balthazar muttered to himself.

Though the cave might be wet and colder than in the field, it gave some protection against both the elements and any other threat. The puffy ruler had asked them to return to him, but a return to the slimy man now seemed inappropriate and wrong—the three kings had briefly discussed a visit to Herod, but quickly purged it from their minds. It was obvious the man had more devious reasons for wanting to know where the boy was. But Jaspar made a valid point as they readied their pallets.

"If we don't return to Herod, I'm worried what he'll do—not to us, but to the infant and his family, certainly," Jaspar stated, cracking his knuckles.

"He'll do nothing—the more I think about it, the more I think he wants us for some strange purpose."

"What would that be, Balthazar?" Melchior asked.

"Well..." he began, thumbing an earlobe. "Perhaps it is some sort of strange test, this time from an earthly man. A test of our authenticity."

Melchior sighed. "What would he test of us? What weakness would he look for?"

"It's a loaded test. It's imbalanced and unfair, surely. Listen," the ruler of Saba said softly, gently raising his hand at Jaspar's rising question. "He knows of the prophecy; surely he knows of Bethlehem."

"He knows the boy is here!"

"Yes, yes, Melchior, he does. He knows the region, in any case. But even if he saw the star, he would not know where to go, and now the star is gone."

"Others may have returned to tell him," Jaspar offered.

Balthazar thought on that for a moment, then shook his head. "Others may also have left by other routes, or…" He trailed off, thinking. The cave was quiet for several minutes before Balthazar's laugh echoed in the small space. "Ha! Exactly, that is the truth!"

"What…?" Melchior wondered.

Jaspar looked on, bewildered.

"It's too simple! What would you say should a peasant come to you and declare that the incarnation of God had been born in a stable surrounded by asses, cows, mules, and shepherds, in a tiny village? What would your answer be?"

"I would—" Jaspar stopped, his face deadpan. "I would find it hard not to laugh them away, unless… unless I—"

"Unless you had seen it!" Balthazar added enthusiastically. "So even if they do tell Herod, he will shoo them away and wait for our response. And that is our problem. What do we tell him?"

"If we tell him we saw the boy in the stable, he will call us liars and mock us."

"Yes, Melchior, yes. I fear for the worst, however. He will call us sorcerers and followers of a false god. Herod would proudly declare that three foreign rulers traveled thousands of miles to worship at the feet of an infant born in a stable. That should be enough to place us in the town square, possibly crucified."

Jaspar shuddered. The Romans seemed to have devised a great number of painful ways by which a man could be executed. "And if we lie to him?"

"What lie would we tell?"

"What if we tell him we did not find the King of the Jews?"

Balthazar sucked in air and the temperature in the cave dropped suddenly. "I would rather not tell that kind of lie, Jaspar."

"It is not entirely—"

"I know what you are saying, that we found the King of Man, the future of the world, God *himself*—by strict definition not the King of the Jews. But, Jaspar," he said, chest heaving, "it is still a lie! Only an hour ago, we walked away from the stable pure of heart. I felt as if every bad thing I had done had been washed away, pulled into that little baby and vacated. And when the mother spoke, I thought I was going to cry the entirety of the great ocean... Now we speak of lies."

"Balthazar, Jaspar does have a point," Melchior said slowly. "Herod might as well be the Devil for the problem he has presented."

"*He* presented? If we had only gone to Bethlehem first, we never…" But Balthazar trailed off. They had no way of knowing where the star pointed—at the time, it made sense to stop in the large city. But, a dark thought crossed his mind. *What if future generations would point to their stop in Jerusalem as evidence of more sinister work? Had they followed the star to its true destination, would it not have led them to Bethlehem in the first place? No,* he reminded himself, *a star is a massive thing, a body as big as the sun. To be as close as twenty miles was astounding—the presence of a huge city could have been, must have been coincidence. The cloud that covered the star, however, surely belonged to the Devil, not the star itself.*

"Well?" Melchior inquired, watching as the myriad of thoughts passed over Balthazar's face.

"It is still not right," the King of Saba said flatly.

"What else could we do?" Jaspar wondered.

"If we leave here, I fear Herod will come and—well, it's a horrible thought."

"He will do just that, Melchior. You can count on it. But he looks the type who would do it no matter the cause. No matter what we do, he will come. Should we warn the citizens of this place?"

"They would laugh at us, call us fools," Balthazar muttered.

"Are we stuck?"

"Stuck, we are, Jaspar. But we can get out of it."

"How?" wondered Melchior.

"Much like the quicksand, my friend. We have to be slow and steady with this Herod. We will return to him and tell him that we did not find a newborn King of the Jews."

"But…" Jaspar protested, mouth wide, fists clenched. "That is surely a lie!"

"It is an omission."

"It is a lie through omission. What's the difference?" Melchior cried.

"As I said, we have to be careful. We can still tell him the entire story. The King of the Jews, we did not find. Truthfully, we found the King of Mankind. Herod would look at us as usurpers and crucify us. No, we tell him that we found only a small baby, born recently, a boy who had many visitors due to his radiant nature."

Melchior snorted. "And the next question that Herod will ask is—"

"'Do you three believe him the next King of the Jews?'" Balthazar answered. "And what would our honest answer be to that question?"

The men stared at him, and mouthed the word *no*.

"The answer, no, it would be. We believe him to be the true Son of God, God himself, Savior of Mankind, not a king merely of one people. With that, I would hope that Herod would let us go. And more importantly," he added, "ignore the boy, and ignore Bethlehem."

"What if Herod does order our deaths?"

"Jaspar, that would be our fate." The response was quick and came with little emotion. Inside their hearts, the warm peace of the Savior radiated calm and acceptance. Such was their fate, should it go that far. The three kings had led when servants should have. They battled the very Devil atop a windy mountain, fought through quicksand, and stepped headlong into the chamber of the vile Herod—each step forward on their travels surely placed their heads that much closer to the noose or cross. They had completed their journey.

The Jaspar who left Tharsis is no longer the Jaspar who is here, or who will be.

"Mourning," was the only word that Melchior whispered.

"Death," Jaspar repeated. "We knew we were going to die, certainly." A thumb knuckle popped. "Then we will die with peace in our hearts."

"Then we will die," Melchior repeated quietly. Their journey had come to an end, an end they had been prepared for. Though their true and possibly horrible deaths on a Roman cross would be agonizing, the sacrifice would not be without reward. The true King of Man had been born. They paid their tribute, offered their blessings, and it was time to reconcile to Herod and pay to man what was due. From God, their payment would be infinite.

They had died.

Balthazar nodded. "Now, let us try to get some sleep before we travel back to Jerusalem."
The men lay down with groans and pops and squeaks from tired joints and muscles. As he lay on his pallet, the King of Saba stared into the darkness, his mind racing. A thought came to him and he immediately rose, grabbed the torch, and excused himself from the cave. The others looked after him, but exhaustion held them firmly in reclined positions. He called out "Nador" as he passed from the cave.

$

Balthazar slipped quietly out of the cave, dashed across the main square of Bethlehem, and searched for Nador among the other retainers. Many were already abed or talking quietly before small fires. The cold night air and access to wood was influential in the lighting of larger and larger fires. A few men and women nodded to Balthazar and he greeted them respectfully. Nador was shrugging into a thick coat when he saw Balthazar and nodded, then crooked an eyebrow, silently asking, *What are you doing here?*

"Come over here," the King of Saba said softly. Nador shuffled over to him and they lowered their heads in hushed conversation. The servant nodded slowly as Balthazar spoke, and when finally their conversation was completed, the men embraced and the king returned to the cave.

Jaspar and Melchior were still awake and reclined on their blankets, heads propped up on their rolled-up robes. Exhausted though they were, neither could find sleep until they knew their companion had safely returned. Balthazar would have thought them sleeping, if he had not seen their flash of their eyes in the meager torchlight.

He quietly readied his own pallet on the floor and lay down with a heavy sigh, joints creaking and popping. The small sounds echoed in the cave, and he was reminded of the sounds his fire had made on the night they saw the star. Coupled with the slowly dying light of a torch he had set into a crevice, the ruler felt warm and at home, though he lay in a damp cave a thousand miles from his palace.

"Is everything in order?" Melchior asked.

There was a pause and finally Balthazar perked up. "Oh, with me? Yes, I told them they should return to Saba in case we..." He trailed off.

Jaspar cleared his throat and changed the subject. "If we were willing to put people on the street, we would have had rooms at the inn."

Melchior snorted. "They didn't move people out of their rooms so that young mother could give birth to her son in a warm, safe place. We're far less worthy of accommodations than he is."

"I know, I know, just an observation."

The cave fell silent and soon Balthazar could hear the soft snores of Melchior as he fell into the darkness of sleep. Soon, Jaspar joined him and the small stone room echoed slightly with pops and wheezes. He had been annoyed by their night sounds during the long journey, but now found himself somewhat comforted by them. They had seen so many strange places and survived under some harrowing conditions—his only friends in the world were by his side and he felt embraced by their presence.

Faces wobbled and bobbed in his mind as his brain began its slow descent into oblivion: Herod, the scholar in Jerusalem, the so-called mayor of Bethlehem, and lastly, the infant child in his ragged swaddling clothes. In his mind's eye, the compressed face of the newborn rotated slowly, illuminated by the bright star. Eventually, it stopped and faced him; then slowly, bright, luminescent eyes opened to reveal small pools of vast intelligence. He felt himself drawn into the baby's eyes, closer and closer until he was pulled into a pillar of pure white light.

The torch guttered with a loud hissing sound and he was wrenched from the experience. Groaning, he rolled over and quickly dove back into the violet, swirling world of sleep, although his next dream was not as pleasant.

Chapter 20
The Dream

And he said, "Hear my words: If there is a prophet among you, I the Lord make myself known to him in a vision; I speak with him in a dream.

Numbers 12:6

Red light flashed in bright, undulating swirls of color. Eyes opened as wide as only a dream can allow, colors distorted, filtered, broken, and misshapen by the shattered stream of thought within sleep. As his limited sight came into weak focus, he found himself standing on hard-packed, crimson sand. Dust whirled and billowed out in cyclones, spinning in all directions, picking up rocks and tossing them against his flesh. He could feel the pinpricks of the sharp gravel as it dug into his bare skin.

A sudden low rumble shook the earth, tumbling mountains and boiling oceans. Chasms opened in all directions, skittering out in a spider web pattern of bottomless caverns and canyons. A resonating voice boomed from all corners of the earth, filling not only his ears, but his mind, speaking directly into his consciousness. Desperately, he searched for the source of the voice, but the dust clouds obscured his vision.

"Beware," the voice warned.

He tried to speak, but his lips pressed firmly together. The voice seemed to come from everywhere and nowhere. As if pulled on strings, the clouds of red dust lifted from the air, pulled completely out of the dream. With this strange event, his vision cleared, and the dull, sandy crimson was replaced by the brown dust of a huge desert. Similar to the one he had crossed with his companions. Far in the distance, a square pillar resolved itself in his vision, and as he scanned its sharp, vertical face of smooth white rock, he startled at the sight of a man. A lone figure stood atop the pillar.

With legs of heavy liquid, he tried to trudge toward the column, but though he strained every muscle, he could not move. This was the second time he had been pressed against an invisible barrier.

Eventually, he managed two steps, but the pillar seemed to have moved. It now appeared several miles across the desert. "I…," he said, his voice thick and warbled in the dream.

"You may approach," came a thunderous reply.

He felt a tingling in his legs, and as he looked down, the rubber appendages had transformed to those of a powerful stallion. Instinctively, he lurched forward, bounding with impossible speed toward the tall structure. With a single leap, he jumped to the top of the pillar. When he landed, he settled in tall, flowing grass that reached his knees.

The man atop the mountain was obscured by a swirling vortex of fog and steam, though glimpses of his head could be seen, but the dreamer could only make out a white beard—or was it simply more of the fog? Again, the resonating voice greeted him, but it was without violence or ill intent. It soothed and reassured, bringing peace and contentment. The dreamer remembered meeting a man atop a mountain, a man of gold, but it seemed a thousand years ago. That man had oozed ill will, desperation, and sickness. The man in his dream was the opposite: Calm, soothing, restful, and warm. "Do not be afraid, my dear Melchior. Do not be afraid."

The king floated forward. Invisible arms embraced him and he at once felt a great relief. An immeasurable burden seemed to float from his shoulders and dissipate in the air around him. "I am not afraid," he whispered.

"I have come to thank you and to give you a warning."

"Thank me?"

"Yes," came the booming reply. "You and your companions have done a great and wonderful deed, and it will surely be remembered throughout history. As for the warning—I do not have much time with you, but you must know this. Look down." A blurry hand pointed down and to the east from the lip of the tower.

Balthazar watched in fascination as the sere land transformed into rolling, hilly country, spotted with rocks and small villages. In one village, he thought he could make out the top of a stable. "Is that...?"

"It is the town you call Bethlehem. Watch."

As Melchior watched, a swarm of beasts topped a rise on the northern edge of town; beasts covered in bright sliver scales, reflecting the brightness of the sun. Extending from their backs were pointed implements, and some had long, gleaming, silver talons. The swarm neared the village, and Melchior realized they were not beasts but men! Soldiers—Roman soldiers, marching quickly!

"Is that happening now?" the king asked in panic, turning to address the man.

"Not yet. But it will. I must go now." The voice faded, and so did its visage—wobbling slightly and then fading away, like a pool of water in the scorching desert. Balthazar looked out at the Roman soldiers as they descended upon the small village of Bethlehem, all their focus not on the manger, but on the cave! From where he stood, he could see the cave, and in the way of dreams, he could even see inside it. Soldiers burst into the space where the men were sleeping, and—

$$\oint$$

He shot awake, slicked with sweat. With the nervous terrors of a dream—no, a nightmare—interrupted he wiped his face and rubbed his eyes with fury, nervous glances darting around the dark cave, looking for any Roman soldiers. When his eyes adjusted, he realized each of his companions was doing the same thing. The sound of labored breathing filled the cave.

"Did you just have a nightmare?" Melchior asked.

"I did." And when Balthazar described it, both Jaspar and Melchior dropped their jaws in wonder. They had each had the same dream, exactly as the Nubian had described it, down to the tall grass atop the pillar.

"Pack quickly," Balthazar ordered. He again wiped sweat from his brow and fumbled for another torch.

"Load the camels and have them ready in the back of the cave. I need to tell my men to go around another way themselves. I'd rather they not wait until we don't show up—it could be too late by then."

"But what about...?" Jaspar asked, eyes wide.

"The risk, I will take." The king shrugged into a dusty robe and ducked out of the cave. Only a few stars shone in the sky and he could see no clouds moving, which meant that dawn was only a few hours away. If their collective dream were true, it would only be a short time before Herod's Centurions found them.

He ran swiftly across the town square, eyes nervously scanning for torchlight, or any other form that didn't belong. As he neared the dark opening that was the village's gate, he sprinted to the eastern side of the opening and flattened himself against the stone wall. With tentative steps, he edged closer to the entryway and peered out into the darkness.

Balthazar stepped out into the desert, constantly looking behind and around him. So far, he appeared to be the only person about at this late, or early, hour. Their caravan had made camp about a quarter of a mile from the gate and he jogged toward the spot. As he neared the small rise before their encampment, he pulled up short and dropped instinctively into a crouch.

A wan light flickered just over the hill, and with it gruff voices and the pleading voice of his servant. Heavy boots scuffled in the coarse ground, the light clang of Roman armor shattered the night, and the whimpering of several servants added to the indecency unfolding.

How dare they!

Balthazar's throat caught. He recognized two of the voices, those of the Centurions they had encountered earlier. Balling his fists, he waddled forward a few paces before flattening himself on the ground. Peering out at the camp below, he ground his teeth in frustration, and tears welled in his eyes.

One of the Centurions held his servant by the scruff of his neck, while the other waved a smoking, flickering torch in his face. The voice was as harsh, gruff, and full of vitriol as it had been in Jerusalem. His gaze lolled from side to side, as if looking for his superiors. Balthazar ducked down when the leering gaze turned far too the left—it only took a brief look in those cold eyes, reflected in the torchlight, to understand that the Centurion was out for blood, regardless of what Nador could say.

"You say you don't know? How can you not know where they are?"

"I—" the man protested.

"Do you know the penalty for lying to a ranking official of the Holy Roman Empire?"

Balthazar nearly choked. These men weren't of any true rank. They were merely thugs! Herod's goons. Surely they had used their purported authority in such a manner before. Their actions now hardly seemed unrehearsed.

Still, against the brusque and coarse threats from the solder, Balthazar's servant held his ground, something the king could at least be proud of. "I am not lying, Centurion. They are, after all, astronomers, followers of the stars. Surely they are out gazing—"

There was a sickening slap as a rough hand met the man's face. "Silence! Do you see any stars? No! I see one or two, hardly any worth looking at!"

Balthazar craned his neck upward, angry at the senseless statement, but the Roman soldier was right— the previous highway of stars was dim, with only a few faint orbs twinkling despondently in the black night.

"I think," the other Centurion said, in an all-too calm voice, a voice that dripped dark thoughts and intended actions. "I think we need to search him. And everything around here. Take everything apart. Search the women." From his cover, Balthazar could see the sneer draw slowly into a malicious smile. "And search them thoroughly, I say. Perhaps they can tell us where these so-called wise men went."

"They are kings!" the man stated.

"Kings, ha! Sorcerers, evil sorcerers. For they brought that dark cloud today. They tricked our great Herod—may his name live forever—into allowing an audience. We've come to find them and bring them to justice! How dare they bring news of a newborn king... There is only one king!"

Balthazar hung his head, his forehead resting on the dry, cold, and dusty rock. He should have known that Herod would waste no time in sending his thugs. That they came for them directly was somewhat of a solace, however. At least they had not found the boy. Or had they? Surely, there would have been a commotion... but how had they discovered that they were in Bethlehem? Or had they simply run into his caravan on their search?

"N-no, please. I tell you, they—"

Another sickening slap. "You have very little time to tell us where they went before we carry out Roman justice."

Nador's cries filled the night air. The man was heaving great, racking sobs.

He is going to give us away. Balthazar wanted to shout, to wave, to call out to his man, tell him it was not a sin to betray their position. They were the leaders, the ones who had risked their lives to travel this distance. Following the star to parts unknown was bound to present risks and challenges, and the last person he wanted harmed was Nador.

He pursed his lips in the beginning of a birdcall, one they had shared as children. A low-pitched warble indicated that there was danger, while the higher-pitched call was one of assurance, that danger had passed. But here on this dusty and rocky plain, any birdcall would alert the Centurions. As soldiers, they would surely know such a call for what it was. Surely they—

They are blind and deaf, a voice echoed in his head.

A tear dropped with a small splash to the ground as Nador was hit once again.

He shook his head, but the voice had been clear. Having survived enough encounters on this journey, he didn't think twice in acting. Balthazar balled his fists and pursed his lips, and piped once in the strange-sounding warble. The guards gave no indication that they had heard. A second after letting out his whistle, Balthazar leapt from his spot and sprinted for the cave. As he sprinted away, he swore he could hear Nador sobbing and the crunch of the Centurions' boots on the hard ground as he bolted into town. Upon hearing the steps of the Roman soldiers, Balthazar pushed his legs faster, not caring who saw him, and bolted through the town square, out the northern gate, and into the dark opening of the cave.

"Go, go!" he bellowed, panting. Upon seeing an empty slab of stone, his heaving heart sank. *They already got them,* he thought. But surely that was an irrational feeling... He raced to the back of the cave where he nearly collapsed from relief.

The others were situated in the far back of the cave, already saddled and ready. Casting a nervous glance behind him, he saw the torchlight bobbing faintly in the town square. As an afterthought, he removed his tunic and dusty robe and tossed them onto the ground—if the Centurions found nothing, they would turn right around and kill Nador and the rest of the caravan. But as long as he left evidence of themselves, he could deflect attention back to his retinue and onto the kings. He hoped it would confirm that the three men *were* out gazing at the stars.

If they could ride hard to the east, away from here, and out of Roman reach, they could escape the Centurions and allow Nador time to flee.

He could only hope.

Torchlight flickered off the wall, and the muted but gruff voices of the soldiers were clear. Balthazar crouched again, then dashed to the rear of the cave, where he veritably leapt atop his camel and kicked it forward. The animal sensed his urgency and flew forward; his companions raced along ahead of him. Though the roar of the hooves against the hard earth drowned out all sound, he swore he could hear the Centurions cursing the empty cave and the single garment left behind.

Chapter 21
A Different Way

But I do as the Father has commanded me, so that the world may know that I love the Father. Rise, let us go from here.

John 14:31

ador's heart was heavy as he watched the Centurions race into the village. The signal from Balthazar was clear—his king was safe. But how safe? It was some distance to their cave, but the soldiers of Herod's army could easily cover that ground—would the three kings be able to make it out to safety, or had his ruler sacrificed himself for the good of those in the caravan? In either case, it was a terrible feeling to know he had betrayed his king and his friend.

You have not betrayed them, a voice chimed in his head. True, Balthazar had lifted his birdcall to the night, the signal of safety. Knowing his ruler too well, however, Nador knew that the kings were far from safe. Again, it was Balthazar who was sticking out his throat for the knife. Nador's king and his companions had seen the star first, had insisted upon leading, and had acted more like rugged adventurers than kings. Safe? No, his ruler, and Jaspar and Melchior, were far from safe—they were putting their lives ahead of Nador's. Ahead of the servants' lives, and ahead of countless others.

He stared at the hulking shadow of Bethlehem when another servant approached. "What do we do now? Should we go after them?" the terrified underling asked.

"No," Nador replied, turning and rubbing his chin where the Centurion had struck him. Strange, for such a well-armed man, the blows were not as forceful as he had expected—nothing strong enough to knock him off of his feet.

"We better leave here and quickly. I think His Majesty will have escaped by now." He sighed, knowing this statement may well have been an utter lie. "We must take our leave before the soldiers return. Let us go south and east, away from here." He shrugged and turned toward the camp, but the man placed a tentative hand on his arm.

"Perhaps—perhaps we can find this city of Tharsis that King Jaspar came from."

Nador's eyes went wide as he regarded the man. "How do you know where this man came from?" Nador wondered. To his knowledge, he had not told anyone the identities of the other kings, for none of the retinue could understand the three men when they talked.

"I listened to them talking."

"But could you understand them?" Nador wondered, incredulous. Perhaps this man had a special gift, or he knew the language the others spoke.

"No, but I heard bits and pieces... Their names were Jaspar and Melchior—er, *King* Jaspar and King Melchior, I should say. I heard those words again and again and thought... well, er, that would be their names."

"Smart man," Nador replied.

"Thank you, sir. I—excuse me, but will the kings be killed?" He wrung his hands.

"I hope not. The birdcall told me that they were safe—if only His Majesty could get back in time, they would have time to escape."

"What about the boy?"

Nador's heart sank. Would the Centurions be so cruel? Could they? He had seen their bravado and his cheeks still stung, but to harm a baby? No. They seemed too eager on finding the kings. Balthazar's friend hung his head and breathed out a silent prayer for the boy's safety.

"Nador... sir?"

"It-it's all right. The boy will be all right," he said, but when he returned the underling's gaze, his eyes were wet. "We must go now."

"I'll get everyone ready."

"Thank you," he said softly and turned to his own tasks.

The caravan was set up and underway in a matter of minutes. Having performed the task countless times on their journey, they were quick and efficient in their work, but the effort seemed hollow, the air duller, the sky murkier, without their three leaders. No words were spoken as the line of servants trudged southward, though many nervous glances were cast backward. Several more stars blinked into being above them as the thin cloud cover faded.

"We cannot return to Saba, I'm afraid," Nador said to the men riding alongside him. "With His Majesty gone, the rebels will surely..." He let the sentence fade away. He could not shake the constant lump in his throat. His king had been a boyhood friend, and even within the boundaries of culture and protocol, Balthazar had been a close companion. To think him gone, either dead, or on a different journey entirely, was disheartening.

"I'm sure they are safe." A man named Salazar spoke.

"I would pray so, too. I wonder where they are going."

"Perhaps they will follow another star?" Salazar wondered.

Nador shook his head. "They followed a very important star—maybe they will travel some more or settle somewhere, but I believe they will not chase stars anymore."

The man coughed. "I see. Well, some of us... some of the others, that is, they—" He hung his head sheepishly and persistently avoided Nador's gaze.

"What? They what? There's nothing to be embarrassed about, surely!"

The man still looked uncomfortable and shifted his weight on the camel. "Some, well, would like to go back and follow this boy. When he gets older, that is."

At that, Nador laughed.

"You said not to be—" The man looked sheepish.

"No, no, of course not! I agree with you!"

"What?"

"Surely. Surely we will return to follow this boy... but he must grow, and we can't stay in Bethlehem."

"You... you want to follow as well?"

"Of course," Nador said softly. "Did you not see the star? How it fell down to earth like that? That was the work of God, if you ask me."

The man beamed. "I saw it too... Who could *not* see that?"

At that, Nador's heart skipped again. If they saw the holy light, then surely soldiers or Herod's men could have seen it, too. From the reactions of the kings, Nador had a sense that Herod...

Had his name been Herod? he wondered. *Balthazar had said as much,* he thought, *but perhaps not...* Still, the kings, Balthazar especially, were scared after their meeting with the man. Unlike Nador's king, Herod surely would be put off by the three kings' presence, by their demeanor. Herod would destroy any threat to his local power—even if it were the newborn king of the world, the Savior. *If he lives, that boy is going to have to be very careful...* "We shall follow him. Perhaps we can help protect him somehow."

"Then that is what we will do."

"That is what we will do," Nador repeated. "Maybe we'll have to change our names, grow longer beards, change our hair, but—"

Encouraged by Nador's agreement, the man perked up. "People won't recognize us when we return, and maybe he'll be in another town altogether by then!"

"Then why change your name?"

"Why not?" Salazar replied. "They will know I am from Saba, with my name..."

"And what would be wrong with that?"

The man scratched his chin. "Well, I don't know exactly, but I feel like I need to start over. With their majesties... with the kings... they have left everything.

They were rich and had land, a lot of land. They just left it. Can you imagine?"

Nador could imagine only a fragment of the kings' plight. He had grown up under semi-privilege, but nothing compared to Balthazar's, Jaspar's, or Melchior's. Wealth, power, land, and influence… the men had vaulted from their pinnacles of power down to the level of the underlings in a single night. Well, it had taken a journey of a thousand miles to reach that pinnacle, but they had each been resolute in their drive to get there. All gone. Everything.

All for an infant. A different king.

Death. Mourning. Sadness. These feelings welled inside Nador, but they were only allowed so much growth, for an overwhelming sense of peace and enlightenment washed over him. He could not fully understand the terms the way the kings did, but he knew that he had passed through an invisible gate, left his prior self in the dust, and had been reborn.

He could not help but laugh in hopeful expectation. "You can change your name, Salazar, surely." A smile spread across his lips and then a sense of elation burst into him, cracking his mouth wide open to reveal his yellowing teeth.

"What is so funny?" Salazar wondered with a smile of his own.

"Oh, I just thought of a name you could use, that's all."

"And what would that be?" he asked leaning over.

Nador sat up straight and patted the neck of his camel. "Oh, I quite like Simon."

$$\oint$$

The torchlight bobbed far behind them and then vanished as they cleared a small rise. They pushed the camels into a dead run for another mile before stopping them completely and dismounting. Both man and beast seemed relieved by the break in the blistering speed—the air filled with clouds of steam from each as they slowly walked into the night.

"We're safe now," Balthazar said, his chest still heaving from the excitement. *But what about Nador?*

"As long as we keep moving, we should be fine… Where are we going anyway?" Melchior wondered.

Balthazar pointed north, then looked up into the sky. "We'll follow the great bear for a while… staying northeast—keeping the Pole Star slightly to the left… and then perhaps we'll go westward. Perhaps not. There is a large sea to the far north, or so I have heard."

The others nodded to themselves. "Do you think Herod's men will pursue us further?" Jaspar wondered.

"It's possible and I would be ready, but they did not strike me as men who would put too much effort into following their prey. No, it's Nador I'm worried about—I hope they took my signal as a clue to leave as soon as those thugs came after us."

"Surely they did," Melchior replied, trying to sound reassuring.

"I would never forgive myself if I was responsible for any harm... any harm that came to any of them. They have been very loyal and trusting—they never saw the star for days and yet they remained with us." He thumbed his earlobe absently. "If anyone is to die at the hands of the Romans, it is I."

Jaspar's instinct was to reject the notion, but in truth, his feelings were closely matched with Balthazar's. And Melchior's certainly. They had been guided by the star, they had laid their gifts at the feet of the next true king—their lives were forfeit, for the greater good, not Balthazar's servants. But as he thought more about the men and women in the caravan, a strange birdcall echoed across the desert. And then there was silence.

"Was that...?" Melchior wondered.

Balthazar shook his head. "No, that was not Nador. That was a real bird."

"It sounded—"

He was interrupted at the sound of hoof beats suddenly drumming on the hardened gravel. Up from behind a narrow valley to their right, two horses emerged, careening across the desert. Men clad in black rode each animal, with one of them bearing a guttering torch. Torch and moonlight reflected off of a nasty cudgel held in a hairy hand.

"That was us," barked the first man as the horses skidded to a stop in front of the kings. Dust plumed into the air.

"Indeed, it 'tis," added the second. "Now, what would three men such as yourselves be doing out in this desert at night? All alone. And unarmed?"

"Unarmed," repeated the first.

"We are but simple astronomers, following the paths of the stars, wondering where each constellation will lead us," Balthazar said flatly, trying to talk down the flutter in his heart.

"Is that so?" The cudgel-bearing man hefted the device and swung it menacingly in the air, leering at the travelers, while the other circled the three camels, poking the torchlight here and there to inspect whatever belongings they may have had.

"They got nothin'."

"Nothin', eh? Well, surely you must have some possessions? Some money? Food? Gold? Else, how far do you think you are going to go?"

"We have a few foodstuffs in these packs," Melchior gestured. He bit his lower lip, then forced his face into an expressionless mask.

"Well, then, what do you think we should do with these... *gentlemen?*" the first asked, brandishing the cudgel. He sneered.

"I think they should be punished for wasting our time."

The man with the cudgel circled the kings slowly, his gaze never leaving the men. Balthazar met his stare flatly and watched with a stiff back as the thug scowled at him, the cudgel held loosely in his hand. "I would agree with that... especially this one," he said, his gaze snapping away from Balthazar to smirk at Jaspar. "He looks dangerous."

"Very."

The first bandit waved his weapon. "Off of your camels, now! Now!"

Grudgingly, carefully, the three kings dismounted and stood together, watching the two thugs. The bandits dismounted, and the torch-bearing ruffian tossed it casually to the ground; the flame guttered but remained low, a tiny sliver of light struggling against the desert dust. He then produced an equally sinister cudgel. Balthazar, Jaspar, and Melchior stood erect, eyes wide, watching in poorly suppressed terror as the ruffians stalked slowly toward them.

We have done good by God, Balthazar thought as he watched the cudgel swing up into the air. *Although death by crucifixion would have been nobler... we still have done our deed.* In the bare moonlight, he could see the end of the weapon was made out of tightly wound hair to which finely sharpened metal spears were attached. The nasty bludgeon was meant not only to pummel, but to cut and pierce. As the bandit brought his arm down to strike, Balthazar's eyes closed, and he waited for the painful onslaught—

"That's enough of that, boys!" came a gruff and familiar cry. A man grunted low in his stomach, his heavy body slammed to the gravel with a rolling, scrabbling thud, followed by another.

Balthazar opened his eyes and was nearly blinded as the area was flooded in torchlight. The beams danced off two lumps on the ground.

Likewise, Melchior and Jaspar let out sighs of relief at seeing their foes tossed to the ground. But even as they welcomed the respite, their breath caught at the sight of their would-be rescuers.

"Ah, it is you three!" came the coarse reply of the Centurion.

Balthazar groaned.

Like being rescued from the belly of the whale by a shark! Jaspar thought.

"Aye, we wondered where it was you went." The second one approached the kings and Balthazar cowered instinctively, then forced himself upright. He expected the slash of steel and the pain of a sword as the Centurion approached, but the man bent down and forcibly removed the robe of the bandit. His companion likewise removed the other's attire.

"Well..." began the second Centurion, hefting the garment. "With that one we found in the cave, plus these two—makes three. How convenient. How very convenient." He rolled them up and stuffed them into a tattered leather pack behind his saddle.

Balthazar tried to calm the trembling in his voice, but failed. "W-what are you—?"

"Aye, not to worry," the leader barked and flashed the barest of smiles. "We have three robes, see? We need three robes to show Herod, don't we?" Upon seeing the look of confusion on the faces of the kings, he waved his hands. "Ach! Well, come on, then, Deltius, let's go... Let these *wise men* figure it out!" He chuckled and showed jagged rows of crooked, broken teeth.

"Aye, Salar," came the gruff reply.

The kings were dumbfounded. *What trickery is this?* Jaspar wondered. A handful of hours prior, these thugs had been eager to beat the men senseless (and, according to Balthazar, they had beaten Nador!), and here they rode away into the night. Doubtful and skeptical eyes watched as the Roman Centurions padded away on their horses.

Here it comes, certainly... Jaspar thought with a scowl as the man called Salar turned about suddenly.

"That was a nice birdcall, by the way," Salar said.

At that, Balthazar nearly choked, but held his face stern. His right hand twitched slightly. With a force of will he kept himself from fingering his ear.

"Ah, don't be so surprised... There's lots of things you don't know about us—much you won't know. Can't a man change? We saw it too," he added with a glance skyward.

"Come on, Salar. Herod will be waiting."

"I'm coming." Before he turned his horse to join his companion, Salar looked back at the three kings. Though his face was only a shadow of a blur in the pale moonlight, Balthazar thought he could see a wide smile on the Centurion's face. But the Roman turned and rode away. In the thin, cold air, the travelers could hear the men talking. Their conversation soon drifted off into silence, but the three kings could make out a few clear words:

"Let's ride hard, Deltius."

"Hey, I told you not to call me that! I told you, after we drop these robes off—"

"Say, wait!" There was the sound of a horse rearing to a stop in the gravel. For a brief moment, the kings worried about another surprise, waited with their breath held in burning lungs. Would the men dare return? What was going on?

"What?" Deltius replied, irritation in his tone.

"Blood! Blind as I was, we'll need to find a rabbit or pig or something, and splash some blood on these things. Make Herod really believe!"

"He'd believe if you just poured wine on them... or, wait, no. He'd smell it. Good idea. We'll find some..."

"Anyway," Salar said, "what were you saying?"

"Aye, stop calling me Deltius. After all of this, I'm going south, going to try my hand at being a merchant. I hear balsam is a good thing to get into... Over Jericho way, I can make my own at it."

"Balsam, eh?"

"Aye, and I'm changing my name, too... so stop calling me—"

"What are you changing it to?"

"Zacchaeus."

"Zacchaeus, eh? Sounds a little puffy for me."

"What do you mean?"

"Well, I..."

The conversation faded into the night, and the three kings stared at each other.

"I..." Balthazar began. He thumbed his earlobe hard enough to crush it into paste.

"There is no other explanation except the boy," Jaspar whispered. "There can be no other."

"They think we don't understand!" Melchior laughed. "Ha!" He bit his lip and laughed again. "I understand perfectly... but I still don't understand!" Laughing again, he threw up his hands. His face was awash with revelation, doubt, joy, rapture, fear, and... relief.

Jaspar smiled. "Perhaps we are not meant to understand. Come, let's ride out of here before these thugs wake up."

Chapter 22
After

For I know the plans I have for you, declares the Lord, plans for welfare and not for evil, to give you a future and a hope.

Jeremiah 29:11

Jaspar sighed and looked out into the purple twilight of the desert. They traveled north and east, following the constellations that led them toward the great sea Balthazar had mentioned. A few times they glanced westward, so used to seeing the brilliant cross-shaped star, but only a single planet and a couple stars punctured the western sky. Several days had passed since they had left Jerusalem behind.

They passed through the cool night for silent hours, following the great bear in the sky. Plumes of steam wafted into the air, hanging in the stillness. Above, the darkening sky was painted with a splashed canvas of stars; soon, the desert came alive with a dull light, as if they were near the entrance of a tunnel and the glow of daylight beyond.

Melchior looked up in time to see a shooting star streak across the violet sky.

The three wise men, magi, kings—whatever names history would call them—pondered both past and future. Their lives were now effectively ended, and their possessions meager, but each felt fuller and richer, and happier even. They had given everything for a journey they hoped would transform.

They had not quite realized that they had been part of a global transformation.

"I wonder if we will be remembered?" Balthazar said softly, smiling.

Jaspar smiled, tears in his eyes. "All that matters is that He is remembered."

As they trotted silently northward, three bright meteors streaked through the atmosphere like huge boulders aflame, blinking once, twice, before splashing against the dark horizon and fading away.

Each man smiled.

THE END

We Three Kings

We three kings of Orient are
Bearing gifts we traverse afar.
Field and fountain, moor and mountain,
Following yonder star.

O star of wonder, star of night,
Star with royal beauty bright,
Westward leading, still proceeding,
Guide us to thy perfect Light.

Born a king on Bethlehem's plain,
Gold I bring to crown Him again,
King forever, ceasing never
Over us all to reign.

O star of wonder...

Frankincense to offer have I.
Incense owns a Deity nigh.
Prayer and praising all men raising,
Worship Him, God on high.

O star of wonder...

Myrrh is mine: Its bitter perfume
Breathes a life of gathering gloom.
Sorrowing, sighing, bleeding dying,
Sealed in the stone-cold tomb.

O star of wonder...

Glorious now behold Him arise,
King and God and Sacrifice.
Alleluia, alleluia!
Sounds through the earth and skies.

O star of wonder...

Afterword

When the idea came to me to write a story about the Three Kings, the first thought I had was to write about their lives *after* visiting Christ. I have been to their gorgeous shrine in Cologne and wondered just how they got there, if indeed they did. The cryptic message from Matthew is simply, "returned to their home by another route." But we never hear from them again, in any history apart from John of Hildesheim. Did they ever get home? History does not provide a good enough answer to that question, though there are several rumors and theories as to where the kings wound up. I'm not sure they ever went back home.

While their journey post-nativity seemed a fascinating opening for a story, the more I thought about it, the more I wanted to describe their trials in getting to Christ. For their actions on that Holy Night were far more symbolic and powerful than many people realize—if I could frame that experience in a harrowing adventure, I felt I could add depth and power to the experience.

The storied Meeting of the Ways is the spot where John of Hildesheim claimed the three kings met one another. Just outside of Jerusalem, this legendary spot has often been sought but never found. Because they traveled together in my story, there was a danger they would miss this historic event, so I made sure they came across the spot and did not miss it.

The legend goes that the kings were interred at the Hill of Vaws and were then moved to Constantinople by Queen Helen. Eventually, Emperor Mauricius got hold of the bodies and took them to Milan, but then Milan rebelled against Frederick the First, and he sent for help, which was granted by Rainald, the Archbishop of Cologne. The Archbishop sent his army and took the bodies back to Cologne, where they lie today.

But are they really there?

It is said that Marco Polo was shown the tomb of the Magi in Persia (Saba, where Balthazar was) and that the tomb was beautiful, with the bodies still whole, hair and beard remaining.

Given the various possibilities for what really happened after they visited Christ, my imagination went wild with possibilities, but the more I thought on it, the more I realized there should still be mystery in where they went after escaping Bethlehem. And escape, they did. Once Herod heard about their leaving, he ordered a massacre—in this fictional story, he may have been upset that the men had been killed, or perhaps he saw through the Centurions' charade. At least Zacchaeus survived, we know, although his story is a bit different.

The kings' actions post-Bethlehem could be exciting fodder for a story, but I think the real story is in how they got there. Or at least the ways in which they could have arrived there. John of Hildesheim says they met randomly in the field and traveled onward as one, but I still like the idea of them knowing each other beforehand and seeing the star collectively. Further, it was important that they saw it before their retainers saw it, in order that we are sure they are the ones being called upon. That their servants stuck with them shows their faith in something—they just weren't sure what.

Additionally, the "pre-journeys" that Melchior and Jaspar endured were vitally important to this story. Their struggles add that much more weight upon the importance of their journey to follow the star, and it highlights the challenges of traveling in ancient times. No GPS and no maps.

Whether you believe that the real Three Kings lie in the cathedral at Cologne or not is up to you. The story is in no way diminished in either reality, because of the impact the men had on the entire world. While some people may feel the need to know that the *actual* Three Kings lie in that golden altar, others can appreciate the symbolism and power of their journey. The true purpose of these brave men was in what they did—not just on their expedition to Bethlehem, but their struggles to even get to each other! Whether they died of starvation in the desert, returned to kingdoms unknown, or simply vanished should not affect the great impact they had upon the nativity story. And upon the world.

For when we see a star that wasn't there, or when we see in our hearts a path we had not seen before, do we have the courage to pack up everything and go? Especially if such action placed you in grave personal danger, if you were forced to forsake the comforts of home, or were faced with the devil himself? These men were rulers of their lands and could, in theory, snap a finger and have people tend to their needs. They could have sent emissaries on their behalf! Instead of lying on soft cushions, they traversed a desert, climbed a mountain, survived quicksand in the moor, outwitted Herod and his Centurions, and presented gifts to the newborn King. These rulers, these kings, kneeled before a little baby in a stable a thousand miles from their palaces.

Where they went after that is not as important as that single act.

I hope you enjoyed this little story and that it opened your eyes and your heart in some way. For within it are many lessons for us and a little humor to keep things steady. When you next celebrate Christmas and the Epiphany, please think about the possible events that I have detailed in here. Hopefully, it will provide for you a deeper appreciation not only of the trials and tribulations of the Three Kings, but of the true meaning of Christmas.

Notes on Terminology

Ancient Navigation – Qiyas and Kalmas

In ancient times, there was no longitude… latitude was the only guide for an ancient seaman. The mariners could use the Pole Star (Polaris), as a measuring tool—called the use of *qiyas:* The seaman held a hand out at arm's length. Four fingers' width was considered 4 isba' (a 360 degree circle had 224 isba'), so a day's sailing to the north moved Polaris 1 isba' from the horizon. By land, the isba' was further divided into 8 *zams*, and land travelers used *zams*.

A kamal was a small rectangular piece of wood that was about an inch by two with a string put through the center. Nine knots were tied along the string, each a specific distance. One held the end of the string in the teeth, and the lower edge of the wood placed on the horizon, while the user moved it until the upper edge touched a desired star. Whichever knot covered the specific distance indicated a given number of isba' of altitude of that star. From this, the altitude of Polaris could be figured.

Ancient travelers did not have the guiding Christmas star at their disposal and so had to navigate by the stars and constellations. It is amazing to think that thousands of years ago, men and women could travel across trackless deserts, without GPS or maps.

Frankincense and Myrrh

I refer to the incense as Frankincense, but that term was not applied until Frankish Crusaders brought it back to Europe. Balthazar calls it olibanum at one point, which is a derivation from Arabic **al-lubān**, meaning "that which comes from milking." It is harvested as described in the book, by slashing the bark of the hardy *Boswellia* tree. The resin oozes out and is let to harden and then is harvested. These trees are so strong they can sometimes grow in solid rock. Frankincense grows in Yemen and Arabia, and its main source in ancient times was in Ubar, Oman.

Again, John of Hildesheim's story is challenged geographically, since Saba is in Persia. However, some historians do claim the fragrant herb originated in Persia, and thus, Balthazar's growing of it is not out of place.

Myrrh is harvested in much the same way, and is native to Yemen, Somalia, and eastern Ethiopia. Jaspar is from Tharsis, a mysterious land, which most likely lay off the coast of Somalia, Djibouti, or Eritrea, where the *Commiphora* trees grow. Myrrh has ancient traditions, from healing Greek soldiers in battle, to domestic trade, and as an ingredient in incenses and cosmetics.

Hill of Vaws

The Hill of Vaws was mentioned in detail in John of Hildesheim's account, and my description follows his template with a little more detail and elaboration. The legend was that twelve wise astronomers were appointed as watchers for the hill and a star that would portend the birth of the King of Men. At this point the old story gets a little confusing, as John describes the Three Kings as erecting the chapel atop the hill. The Kings left by mysterious means in my story, but I still wanted to have them involved in the Hill, and I added the prologue and epilogue to tie the two together.

Since the Hill was the highest point in the region, it stands to reason it would provide a majestic panorama of stars, and thereby would also provide a view of the Christmas star like no other.

Magi

In my story, these men were not magicians or sorcerers. But that portrayal has been one that history has left us in a few forms. One of the very early church authors, named simply Origen (born c. 185 AD), wrote quite an interesting piece on the Three Kings in his text Contra Celsus. He claims the kings were indeed sorcerers, full of evil magic and power, and once they met with Jesus, the evil spirits fled in the presence of God. And so they were transformed and gave their offerings.

The term magi derives from the Old Persian word *magus* and is related to the religious caste of Zoroaster. *Magi* refers to the priestly sect of Zoroastrianism, and these priests were particularly well-versed in astrology. Some scholars argue that the men were astronomers, not astrologers, a notion that I hold dearer to—they were definitely not sorcerers. Ancient man was quick to judge the new and unusual in a darker light, and three men arriving from a thousand miles away might give one the impression that some sort of magic was involved. It is sad that the early church writers had to paint such a picture of the Three Kings; in my opinion, it cheapens the experience and makes them seem less than they were.

Names of the Kings

There are many different variations on the names of the kings, and since they are not named in Matthew, we can never be fully sure of their authenticity or veracity. But names we must have, else the story falls on its face! Balthazar has been written Balthasar, Balthassar, Bithisarea. In the middle English (ʒ) can be taken as an s or z sound, so I used Z, mainly because it imparts a little aura of mystery to the man. Jaspar is often known as Caspar, although Jaspar, Jaspas, Gathaspa, etc. have also been used). Variants of Melchior include Melchyor, Melichior. For this book, I have kept true to John of Hildesheim's spellings, mostly. Hildesheim named Jaspar *Iaspar,* the I converting to J in our vocabulary, and it is easier to pronounce with the J.

Although I have given them the original names, one must question if these are given names or surnames? Since there is very little historical record of these men, we do not have lineages to trace, and thus, we cannot research their true origination. This is not necessarily a bad thing, however, since it is their actions that speak louder than any name. Typically, a powerful king would flaunt his name, embellish it, even add to it. Yet these men went by simple names.

References/Resources

The following resources and references may provide some further interesting reading on the subject.

CanBooks. (2002). Ancient sailing and navigation. Retrieved March 21, 2012 from http://nabataea.net/sailing.html.

Franks Casket. Retrieved April 5, 2012, from http://www.franks-casket.de/english/front02.html.

Hastings, J. (Ed.). *A Dictionary of the Bible: Volume II (Part II: I – Kinsman), Volume 2.*2004, Reprinted from the 1898 version.

Joannes, of Hildeshiem, d. 1376; Horstman, Carl (Ed.). *The Three Kings of Cologne: An Early English Translation of the "Historium Trium Regum".* Published for the Early English Text Society by N. Trübner. London. http://www.archive.org/details/threekingsofcolo00joanuoft.

Kehrer, H. (1908). *Die Heiligen drei KDie Heiligen drei Koenige in Literatur und Kunst.* E. A. Seemann, Publisher.

Origen. *Contra Celsum* I.60 Retrieved April 5, 2012, from
http://www.newadvent.org/fathers/04161.htm.

Stone, C. (November/December, 1980). We three kings of Orient were. *Saudi Aramco World, 31*(6). Retrieved January 8, 2012 from http://www.saudiaramcoworld.com/issue/198006/we.three.kings.of.orient.were.htm.

World Agroforestry Centre, AgroForestryTree Database. *Commiphora myrrha.* Retrieved March 21, 2012, from
http://www.worldagroforestrycentre.org/sea/products/afdbases/af/asp/SpeciesInfo.asp?SpID=17990.

Share the Adventure

If you enjoyed this story, please tell your friends, relatives, your pastor, priest, anyone who you may feel will enjoy this adventure. Buy copies and give to your church library; donate copies to local shelters, small bookstores, etc.

The lessons within this story are important to all of us, and although it is an adventure, it is also a type of sermon, a lesson for us to find our star and pray to God for inspiration and support as we follow. Three very wealthy men gave everything to God—*everything...* and they didn't even know fully what they followed!

This book was written for anyone who enjoys a good Christmas story, an inspirational tale, or grand journey. Most of all, it was written to share the inspiration I feel when I read the story of the Three Kings, the call to follow my star, to serve others and give what you have to those who have less.

I encourage you to spread the word and share the tale. God Bless.

15744574R00168

Made in the USA
Charleston, SC
18 November 2012